Ernest Temple Hargrove

World politics

Ernest Temple Hargrove

World politics

ISBN/EAN: 9783744728836

Printed in Europe, USA, Canada, Australia, Japan

Cover: Foto ©Suzi / pixelio.de

More available books at **www.hansebooks.com**

WORLD POLITICS

BY

"T"

NEW YORK
R. F. FENNO & COMPANY
9 and 11 East 16th Street

London: SAMPSON LOW, MARSTON & COMPANY, Limited
St. Dunstan's House, Fetter Lane, Fleet Street, E.C.
1898

Copyright, 1898,

BY

R. F. FENNO & COMPANY.

All rights reserved

Contents.

PART I.
INTRODUCTORY.

CHAPTER	PAGE
I.—The World's Outlook,	9
II.—A Search for Causes,	19

PART II.
GENERAL CONSIDERATIONS.

III.—What is Sound Policy?	29
IV.—The Nature and Relations of a State,	37
V.—Laws of Life,	43
VI.—Principles of National Conduct,	52
VII.—The Promise of Recent Practice,	62
VIII.—The Lessons of the Centuries,	69

PART III.
PARTICULAR CONSIDERATIONS.

IX.—A Test of Progress,	77
X.—The Evolution of State Law,	84
XI.—The Evolution of International Law,	95

PART IV.

A Practical Measure.

CHAPTER	PAGE
XII.—Its General Character,	105
XIII.—Its First Clause,	108
XIV.—Its Second Clause,	119
XV.—Its Third Clause,	124
XVI.—Some Possible Objections,	136
XVII.—Conclusion,	145

NOTES.

Note A., from p. 40.—A Nation an Organism, . . 155
Note B., from p. 45.—Unselfishness, ... 163
Note C., from p. 49.—The Morality of the Evolutionary Process, ... 165
Note D., from p. 58.—'Splendid Isolation,' or the Interdependence of Nations, ... 167
Note E., from p. 73.—Christianity, ... 181
Note F., from p. 109.—The International Marine Conference, ... 184
Note G., from p. 135.—Sully and Kant, . . . 187·
Note H., from p. 152.—The English-Speaking Peoples. 194

ADDENDUM.—The Czar's Plea for Peace, . . . 203

Part First.
INTRODUCTORY.

WORLD POLITICS.

CHAPTER I.

THE WORLD'S OUTLOOK.

WHAT are the prospects of the world's near future? Are they as gloomy as would appear at first sight? These are questions that the ordinary person has been content, until recently, to leave unanswered; and even now there are those who do not think it worth while to bother their heads with such matters.

It has been asserted frequently that a very large number of people never really think; that they will not face facts which surround them constantly, but which they persistently ignore, until, taken unawares by circumstance, they find themselves driven to immediate action in relation to some fact they have never observed before. Then they hasten to do something, anything, to relieve the situation, when it is perhaps too late, and when ordinary foresight would have spared them a catastrophe.

Men will live near swampy ground, in a hot climate, without giving a thought to their danger, until fever threatens to deprive them of their best beloved. So there are many who never give a thought to the condition of the world around them. They can get along for the moment without serious inconvenience; they have their own affairs to attend to; time enough for the world when its condition affects them personally.

That they must of necessity be affected by it already, and that in a day or a year the danger near which they live may quite vigorously affect them, are facts they do not appreciate. If they imagine they are beyond the reach of other men and other nations, that they are separate from the rest of the human race, they are woefully deceived. If they could completely isolate themselves in the ocean of surrounding nature, it would be a miracle which the most skilful chemist has to confess himself unable to perform; and if they could free themselves from all dependence upon their fellows, they would reverse the experience of many thousands of years.

When Rome fell, not a villager in Gaul remained unaffected. One vote in a House of Legislature, involving the increase or the decrease of some import duty by a fractional percentage, may throw thousands of men out of employment, at home or abroad. A poor employee in an English mill may suppose that the politics of the United States is no concern of his; but in consequence of the Civil War in America, the scarcity of cotton nearly ruined the English manufacturers, and reduced many families in the north of England to abject misery. All classes, no matter what their trade or occupation, are affected by events occurring on the other side of the globe.

It would be wise, therefore, for every one to give some consideration to the condition of the world at the present time, and to endeavour to recognize things as they are, whether agreeable or disagreeable; if possible, to determine the laws controlling the occurrence of the facts observed. If the condition of things be found ideal, the inquiry need go no further. If, on the other hand, matters be seen as capable of improvement, each individual can decide for himself whether he can do anything to improve the conditions: first, for his own sake, if his personal welfare concerns him chiefly; secondly, for the sake of others, if the welfare of others is to him a matter of secondary importance.

It remains to be settled, then, whether the prevailing conditions are capable of improvement.

Even a cursory view of the situation will probably oblige the most persistent optimist to admit that the world's outlook is not exactly promising. Home affairs are bad enough. Friction between

Capital and Labor is a constant menace to the prosperity of nearly every civilized country. Strikes are continually threatened, and often take disastrous effect, injuring the interests of all the parties concerned. Capital combines, Labor combines, and conflict seems inevitable.

A famous French novelist—*before* getting into difficulties with his Government—attributed to one of his characters the following summary of the political situation in France:

"Toutes les questions se rapetissaient à la seule question de savoir qui, de celui-ci, de celui-là ou de cet autre, aurait en sa main la France, pour en jouir, pour en distribuer les faveurs à la clientèle de ses créatures. Et le pis était que les grandes batailles, les journées et les semaines perdues pour faire succéder celui-ci à celui-là, et cet autre à celui-ci, n'aboutissaient qu'au plus sot des piétinements sur place, car tous les trois se valaient, et il n'avait entre eux que de vagues différences, de sorte que le nouveau maître gâchait la même besogne que le precédent avait gâchée, forcément oublieux des programmes et des promesses, dès qu'il régnait."

With some modifications, could not the same conclusions be drawn from the conduct of affairs in other countries claiming, as France claims, to be pre-eminently civilized?

THE WORLD'S OUTLOOK. 13

Turning to international relationships, the world's outlook would appear to be even less encouraging. Nations armed to the teeth, to protect themselves from each other, all declaring that their most ardent desire is for peace! Apart from the direct expenditure of almost incalculable sums yearly on the maintenance of armies and navies, with a resulting burden of taxation almost heavier than the people can bear, the energies of millions of men throughout the world are constantly diverted into non-productive channels, into channels where nothing accumulates. Meanwhile children toil in factories, and thousands of families starve to death, year after year, for want of bread.'

[1] Germany, with a national debt of some 2,000,000,000 marks, spending over 500,000,000 marks a year on its army and navy, maintaining over 600,000 men in arms on a peace footing—men drawn from the ranks of the Empire's workers, converted from producers into fighting automata, for the protection of the Fatherland from France, or Russia, or some possible combination of the Powers.

France, in order to protect itself from the possible aggressiveness of Germany, or for other purposes, maintaining an army of nearly 600,000 men on a peace footing, with 40,000 more in the navy—leaving women who should be mothers to do the work of men. France, with a total debt of about 32,000,000,000 francs, largely the cost of past wars, doing little with its wonderful resources but prepare for another!

Great Britain, spending over £40,000,000 annually on its army and navy, with a debt of over £621,000,000.

The United States, indebted to the extent of $915,962,000,

True, wars are not frequent; but at the first threat of war—such threats being frequent enough—money markets fluctuate, affecting the price of food, of cotton, iron, and every necessity of life, changing the purchasing power of the wage-earner's pittance. Nor does the actual infrequency of war make the sort of peace which prevails any the more tolerable. The equipment for defence makes the absence of war almost more oppressive and more destructive of internal prosperity than open hostilities. War is often welcomed as a relief from the tension and uncertainty preceding its occurrence.

And why is all this necessary? "The better to preserve peace," we are told by some; "To defend ourselves from possible attack," say others. But the absurdity of such excuses as reasons must be

expending some $83,500,000 a year for purposes of defence, but obliged to increase this sum enormously on the first outbreak of hostilities, and paying $141,000,000 every year in pensions as a result of the Civil War. (See *The Statesman's Year-Book* for the above figures.)

Russia's army, on a peace footing, is variously estimated, the numbers given ranging from 870,000 to 1,700,000 men. According to *The Armies of To-day*, Russia spends thirty-five per cent. of its whole public revenue for military purposes.

Reliable authorities state that the six great European Powers could put at least 12,000,000 trained men into the field in case of war, for the armies on a peace footing constantly change their *personnel*, owing to the system of conscription and short service during the prime of life.

patent to every one in view of the facts, and the facts speak for themselves, at once abominable and pitiable in the extreme.

The history of the race, so far as it has been recorded, shows an unceasing strife between the nations. At first sight it would seem that the survival of the fittest has meant little else but the survival of the strongest. Nations have arisen, beginning their self-aggrandisement by overcoming their immediate neighbours; and, pushing on relentlessly to still greater victories, they have finally ruled the world. Then, from this point of view, Time, the great destroyer, has stepped in to do its work, and these dominating nations, first one and then another, have been broken on its wheel, leaving scattered remnants, the prey of ascending powers. So to-day we see some nations struggling desperately to maintain their own predominance, others to gain supremacy in their turn, all in arms against each other—victims of themselves.

Civilization in a *cul-de-sac*, has been the comment of pessimistic observers; though many people are so accustomed to these every-day surroundings that they never think of possible improvement, hardly realizing the need of it. Yet it were better, not only to recognize existing facts, but to seek for their explanation, since these facts concern every one, affect every one, and could be affected by every one.

A rapidly increasing number of people are beginning to understand this, sometimes because the condition of the world is evidently and even obtrusively affecting their personal interests, and sometimes because they see that herein they have a duty to perform. They have for long studied the laws of health in relation to the human body, and now they are seeking for the laws of health which govern nations, obedience to which may conserve a nation's life.

The last few years have seen a great change in this respect. Formerly, foreign affairs were supposed to be beyond the ken of any but cabinet officers and a few select members of legislative assemblies. To-day, the details of international occurrences, whether they be wars or treaties of peace, are fully reported in the press, and are discussed by tens of thousands of both thinking and unthinking readers in every part of the world.

So it happens that remedies for the world's disease of armament are occasionally proposed. One is that a hugely destructive international war would clear the atmosphere and tend to promote peace by provoking a reaction against war. But history warrants no such supposition. On the contrary, universal experience has amply proved that one war leads to another; that a defeated nation is a nation awaiting revenge, and that a victorious nation is a nation awaiting further conquests.

Another remedy which finds support is the voluntary and complete disarming of all the nations of the world, on the ground that war is fundamentally and invariably wrong. Supposing this to be so, it is evident that the nations are not prepared to accept the idea as a correct proposition, even in the abstract; much less are they prepared to act upon it in the way proposed. From no point of view is the remedy feasible, and the theory upon which it is based is open to serious objection, inasmuch as the strong, from an ideal standpoint, will always feel it their duty to protect the weak, so long as the weak need protection, and this may involve the use of force—war in some form or another. A community of saints or sages could alone afford to dispense with violence, and even they might occasionally backslide into employing it. The furthest one can go in this direction is to say that the use of force should be reduced to a minimum. But how this minimum is to be arrived at is another matter.

To submit disputes between states to arbitration is widely suggested as the only means of relieving the international situation. The chief objection to this method is that the result of arbitration, as heretofore conducted, is in no way binding upon the parties concerned, and is liable to lead to a bloodier war than might otherwise have taken place. The partial and temporary damming of a river—in this case of anger or revenge—must always involve a tremendous addition to its volume and destructive power whenever the dam is swept away. So while arbitration is occasionally a palliative, it cannot be regarded as a cure, for it would not lead nations to reduce their armaments: they would want to fall back upon them in case the arbitrator's decision should not meet with their approval.

CHAPTER II.

The World's Outlook and a Search for Causes.

CORRECT diagnosis is necessary if a malady is to be cured. Causes, not effects, must be dealt with. So, if the condition of the world is found to be unsatisfactory and its outlook unpromising, and we would attempt to improve its condition and brighten its outlook, we must seek for the cause of existing circumstances in the line of policy being pursued, and must deal with the cause direct. For although the present international situation is evidently the result of a series of actions performed by governments and peoples, these actions of all kinds, producing both good and bad results in varying degree, spring from a mental conception or policy. This policy is the outcome of a certain attitude of mind.

Thought and desire are expressed in action, action being an effect, not a primary cause. If one man strikes another, the blow results from a thought, perhaps of irritation or anger. It is also true that actions react upon the mind, but no matter what relation "mind" may bear to "matter," or *vice versa*, it is evident that it is in the mind that man suffers and enjoys, and that it is in his mind that all his actions directly or indirectly originate. In other words, in order to change a man's actions it is necessary to change his attitude of mind, replacing one desire with another.

It follows that if we would change the acts of nations we must endeavour to change their policy, first determining what that policy is, and then seeing if it can be replaced by a new policy with practical advantages over the old one. It is always easier to criticise than to create, to destroy than to construct; and although the results so far obtained from the old policy can hardly be considered satisfactory, if no better suggestion should be forthcoming, and if its further trial be likely to promote the prosperity of nations and to increase the happiness of the individuals composing the nations, it should undoubtedly be persevered with at all costs. On the other hand, its results being so evidently undesirable, should the policy in itself be judged mistaken or narrow, it would be foolish to persevere with it. The importance of deciding the question can hardly be disputed.

What the old and still-continued policy is, has been freely admitted by every one: it is the sole duty of all governments to promote the prosperity of the country they represent. In order to do this it is generally considered necessary to increase a country's power and influence by adding to its territory whenever possible, with a view to providing an outlet for its surplus population and to securing additional markets for its surplus produce. Whether by territorial expansion or otherwise, it is in any case deemed to be the duty of a government to promote its country's welfare by practically every means, except at the cost of national dishonour.

The limitations imposed by this care for a country's honour are somewhat indefinite however. The honour of a nation and the honour of an individual are two widely different things. For three strong men to waylay and confiscate the property of a weak man would commonly be regarded as an exceedingly dishonourable act, to put it mildly. Yet it is not inferred that the three nations that partitioned Poland in 1795 really dishonoured themselves by so doing, any more than it is considered that the nations now partitioning China should no longer be regarded as honourable on that account. To extort extravagant interest on a loan to a friend would be condemned as disgraceful. A government, on the other hand, that failed to obtain the highest possible interest on a loan to a friendly nation, or the largest possible concession for services rendered or to be rendered, would be blamed for incompetence.

Various attempts have been made to account for this disparity between the accepted standards of national and of individual morality, the simplest explanation of the incongruity lying in the representative character of a government.

In the narrower field of personal enterprise the zeal of a conscientious agent is apt to run into extremes of cupidity of which a principal would not be guilty. It is supposed that a man can afford to be just, and perhaps generous, on his own account, but when acting for another he should be strictly "business-like" — with consequences dependent upon his own interpretation of the word. From the ordinary point of view, and using words attributed to a well-known statesman, because "a foreign minister is in the position of a trustee, and his highest if not his sole duty is to push and protect the interest of his client, the nation, he must be selfish, more selfish even than a gentleman would be in private life." Hence it is that to speak of an "unselfish statesman" would be almost a contradiction in terms, though unselfish individuals are frequently met with and are everywhere respected.[1]

Meanwhile it is painfully evident that the moral standard of a nation, acting through its represent-

---

[1] For both ancient and modern views concerning the morality required in statesmanship, see Lord Acton's "Introduction" to Burd's edition of *Il Principe*.

atives, is lower than the average standard of these representatives acting in their personal capacities, and that the honour of a state cannot be seriously impugned so long as it is willing to fight any other state not more than twice as big as itself. Hence the efforts made by most, if not all governments, to promote the prosperity of their respective countries, may be summarized as attempts to get all they can and to give or pay as little as they can, without any regard whatever for the welfare of their neighbours, who are supposed to be able to look after their own interests, and to do this in the same way and with the same object in view.

At the same time, and in order to check indiscriminate and inordinate self-aggrandisement by any one nation, the European Powers have asserted that the "Balance of Power" must be maintained, though it may appear strange that states pursuing what has been called a policy of grab should take steps to limit its consequences. Is it possible that each of them hopes to escape the limitations it attempts to impose upon others? For the Balance of Power means the preservation of a kind of equipoise between the nations in order to prevent too great an increase of territory on the part of any one of them.

It is as if all the members of a community whose aim it is to increase their individual wealth by every possible means, regardless of one another's interests, were to agree among themselves that they would not allow any one of their number to get more than he might happen to own already, unless all of them could increase their capital proportionately. A somewhat curious, not to say a bewildering scheme, from that point of view.

It is not surprising that the Balance, first established in the Treaties of Westphalia and Utrecht of 1648 and 1713, and to which so many *salaams* have since been made, has been continually disturbed and more than once entirely upset. It could not prevent the acquisition of territory by genuine hereditary rights; nor could it prevent treaties of alliance between neighbouring states; nor did it originally contemplate the acquisition of territory by *bona fide* colonization. Now that it is past restoration, many statesmen see the fallacy of the theory upon which it was based.

But the policy of self-aggrandisement at any price except loss of national "honour," of which the Balance of Power was in a sense the syzygy, has not yet been abandoned by the European nations, though here and there an unusually enlightened Minister frankly confesses himself dissatisfied with its results and doubtful of its morality.

Such uncertainty is most inopportune, for rarely has there been more need of a well-defined plan of procedure than at present. Vast stretches of territory in Asia and in Africa remain unclaimed, or are without owners able to maintain their rights by force—which amounts to the same thing from the standpoint of current international ethics. Most of the European Powers are encroaching upon these territories as rapidly as decency permits, and one encroachment leads to another, as well as to constant friction and jealousy.

In Europe itself the danger of disturbance is hardly less imminent, for old and formerly powerful nations are beginning to crumble; and though their parts are vigorous enough, the question will soon arise as to whether they are to be allowed an independent existence or whether they are to be merged into other states.

Uncertainty at such a time is fatal, and yet uncertainty exists among the most experienced and reliable statesmen, whose action is naturally vitiated by doubt, and who go on increasing their country's armaments with only the haziest notion as to why and for what these armaments should be used.

Nor is this uncertainty confined to Europe. In the United States also, the gravest doubts are entertained concerning the foreign policy to be pursued. For the seclusion which America has endeavoured to preserve in the past has been violently interrupted, and while some of its people desire to see their country stand aloof from the rest of the world and to return to its former condition of isolation, others urge that it should take its place among the Powers as an expansive and acquisitive commonwealth. There are also those who seek to discover a middle course between what they regard as these two unwise extremes.

It is perfectly evident that the career of a man who has no positive aim in life is not likely to prove successful. A clear-cut purpose, instigating all a man does, will almost insure the attainment of his object. And the same holds true of nations. If they have no definite "aim in life," no settled policy, they will have no chance in the struggle for existence with a nation whose goal is always in sight.

So it is a matter of vital moment to arrive at an understanding in regard to the best policy to be pursued, not only because prevailing conditions are so unsatisfactory, and the world's outlook—seemingly, at least—is so unpromising; but because in no other way can consistent instead of spasmodic and conflicting action be made practicable.

Part Second.
GENERAL CONSIDERATIONS.

CHAPTER III.

What is Sound Policy?

THE merits of a policy can be decided by approaching the subject either deductively or inductively. The policy can be considered in the abstract, in relation to principle, or it can be judged by its effects. Both methods should be followed if reliable conclusions are to be reached.

A perfectly correct statement of principle is a statement of a law of nature or fundamental truth, ascertained as the result of experience. A law of nature—regardless of its origin, whether divinely enacted or innate, a point which does not alter the fact now under consideration—is a statement of the sequence or regular method by which certain phenomena or effects follow the activity of certain forces, material or mental.

Granted the same conditions, certain given causes will invariably produce certain given results. The application of heat, up to a certain degree, will tend to bring about the expansion of the object treated; beyond that degree, heat will cause contraction. This is one of the common physical laws, knowledge of which has come from experience and experiment.

In the domain of the mind, certain laws are easily recognizable. Every strong emotion is followed by a reaction to the other pole of that emotion. In the case of a nervous subject, intense exaltation is followed by intense depression; and if on no other grounds, self-control is seen to be advantageous, so that extremes and their consequent reactions may be avoided.

In nearly every department of life certain general laws are known to hold good, and people conform to them, though often without recognizing them as such, unaware of the fact that they are to that extent acting on principle.

In the political world the administrators of most civilized countries have learned that it is better to govern with a light hand than with severity. A riot might be quickly suppressed by the slaughter of all those taking part in it, but summary treatment of this sort has been found to be injudicious, being likely to provoke further and worse rioting; and as soon as this conclusion had been reached, it came to be seen that a reckless use of force and a brutality of repression were contrary to right ethics. So, though it took many centuries of experience to prove it, it is now usually recognized as a principle of government that moderation should be exercised in dealing with the governed, and that justice should be tempered with mercy or at least with self-restraint.

The aboriginals of Tasmania had been exterminated to a man after the British had occupied the island for less than seventy years. But their ill-treatment occurred many years ago, as did the ill-treatment of the Indians by Americans. Since then, as the result of experience, there has been a radical change of policy in relation to native races, and to-day they are protected by every means possible, evidence of which is found in such legislative measures as the Glen Grey Act of Cape Colony, and in the care now bestowed upon the North American Indians by the United States Government.

It came to be recognized that native races had a distinct *value*, for purposes of labour and as purchasers; that it therefore *paid* to protect them, as they could not always protect themselves; and concurrently with this conclusion came the acceptance of the fact that it was bad enough to rob them of their land, and that to rob them of liberty and life as well was to outrage every known principle of justice. Hence it is now admitted as a principle of colonial government that a certain duty is due to the aboriginal peoples of the countries occupied—a reversal, as said, of the earlier policy, which treated them as interlopers or as slaves.

The world learns slowly. It has to suffer before it learns. It has to go on suffering until by the very pressure of its pain it is obliged to review its actions and the prompting policy, to find them both egregiously foolish as a rule. If, in the first place, the principle of justice had been observed in the treatment of native races, the loss of thousands of valuable lives as well as of much wealth— lives and wealth of conquerors as of conquered— would have been obviated. If the British administrations of the Duke of Grafton and of Lord North had observed the principle of justice, the United States and Great Britain might have been a united people to-day. But might and right have so greatly outbalanced duty, the immediate object to be gained has so greatly obscured consideration of the future, that principles have been lost sight of, and a short-sighted expediency has generally served to instigate action.

The whole question is really very simple. It resolves itself into a choice between temporary benefit and permanent benefit. In order to obtain the permanent benefit it is sometimes necessary to make a temporary sacrifice; and this, people do not always care to do, largely because they doubt the truth of the principle by the observance of which the greater benefit may be secured, while they doubt the truth of the principle because they ignore facts and the lessons of the past until through their own suffering these force themselves upon their notice.

"The supposed antagonism between expediency and principle has been pressed further and further away from the little piece of true meaning that it ever could be rightly allowed to have, until it has now come to signify the paramount wisdom of counting the narrow, immediate, and personal expediency for everything, and the whole, general, ultimate, and completed expediency for nothing. Principle is only another name for a proposition stating the terms of one of these larger expediencies."[1]

This truth is not sufficiently appreciated by many, who perhaps do not understand what a "principle" implies. They are careful to examine the foundation on which they propose to build a house; they know that a foundation of rock is better than one of sand; but they do not apply the same rule universally, and will plunge headlong into action without waiting to examine the basis of their action or its probable ultimate result. They allow themselves to be actuated by the hope of immediate results, either ignoring ultimate re-

[1] *Compromise*, p. 6, by John Morley.

sults, or willing to risk all possible consequences in order to realize their present desire.

To do the right thing, at the right time, and in the right place, is the whole science of life. And to do the right thing involves much more than is commonly supposed. The *right* thing is not only what is ordinarily called the moral thing, but the wise thing to do from every conceivable standpoint; and as wisdom's chief constituent is an understanding of the laws of life, to do the right thing is to act in conformity with universal law.

People sometimes lose confidence in the practicality of doing the right thing, even in the above wide sense, because they are apt to abandon their principle at the first hint of failure. They change the basis of their action, and, forgetting that it often takes time for satisfactory results to develop if these are to be permanent, they debar themselves from ultimate success by descending to some wrong expedient in order to change the current of events and insure instant but passing benefits. When these passing benefits disappear, they attribute their failure to their attempt to act upon principle—which they at once condemn as unpractical—oblivious of the fact that they have not been consistent in their action, and that they changed their course in the middle of a specific manœuvre, abandoning principle, and reverting, through fear, to their customary scramble for quick returns at any price.

If this be sometimes excusable in the case of an individual, acting for himself, who may perhaps lose his head in the swirl of events, it would not be excusable for a general commanding an army to do likewise; and it would be still less excusable for a government controlling the destinies of a nation to be actuated by motives which would disgrace an individual, if it were not that deliberate action is the exception rather than the rule among men.

In the case of a government, it is now supposed, for the better elucidation of the argument, that it has not only the desire, but that it has sufficient strength of will to enable it to do the right thing, once the right thing is known. Any government would claim this much for itself, making it necessary to take it, to that extent, at its own valuation.

In view of these considerations, it is of real importance to discover what general laws or fundamental principles should govern the relations of states. Once these principles are determined, it would be as foolish not to guide a nation's conduct accordingly, as it would be foolish to try to ignore the fact that fire burns; for if one tries to ignore that fact, one suffers, and suffers needlessly. And if one ignores true principles, which are statements of fact, one invites disaster, instead of using such facts as infallible guides to happiness, progress, and peace.

CHAPTER IV.

The Nature and Relations of a State.

BEFORE attempting to discover the laws which govern international relationships and the principles upon which action in connection therewith should be based, it is necessary to realize that this field of human activity is a department of life as a whole; that it is not subject to unique conditions or separable from other kinds of human endeavour and industry.

There are those whose object it seems to be to divide the universe into fractions, constructing a pill-box theory of things in general, labelling each box with elaborate and conscientous care. Even those who should know better not infrequently fall victims to this common craze—the craze for specialization, with partitions between the innumerable departments: Science, tending to become a science of little pieces.

It is not a rare occurrence to find a physician who has become a specialist attributing every malady he encounters to some abnormal condition of that part of the bodily organism he has endeavoured to make his own. A musician, versed in the laws of harmony, familiar with the vibratory theory of sound, will not often seek for some possible connection between vibrations of sound and vibrations of colour, because, forsooth, he has his own department to deal with, and is neither painter nor physicist; nor will he stop to study the effect of different sounds and combinations of sounds upon the nervous system and the mind, although his life is largely devoted to playing upon these living instruments by means of the musical tones he produces. An exponent of religion will consider it sufficient to understand his own, and about the last thing in the world he usually seeks to discover are points of contact between his own and other beliefs.

On all sides there is this tendency toward segregation; and while it is widely admitted to be a danger, and the best minds of the day are constantly pointing it out, it will doubtless take years to change the present marked propensity of human thought and to emphasize adequately the importance of synthesis as well as of analysis, and the need of broad generalization as well as of particular investigation. "To see unity in diversity is to see God."

Hard and fast partitions have not been discovered, separating one department of nature from another, and until they are, we can afford to speak of nature as continuous. For purposes of thought it is useful to specify classes and categories, species and types, races and families; but it would be unwise to regard them as separate in any absolute sense. Certain general laws have been determined, governing all the departments of nature known to us; and as exceptions to these laws have not been discovered, we can afford to speak of them as universal.

One of these universal laws is that of growth. Nothing in nature is stationary. Dissolution and decay are reactionary processes in the vast sweep of an all-embracing development. Everything is subject to this law; and if we could understand the process by which any one part of nature grows at each stage of its development, we should understand the growth of all its parts.

> "Little flower—if I could understand
> What you are, root and all, and all in all,
> I should know what God and man is."

If, then, we could understand the physical, mental, and moral development of an individual, we should understand the physical, mental, and moral development of a nation, of which the individual is a part. All that we know positively of the one, we know of the other.

A human being is said to be an entity consisting, roughly speaking, of (1) a physical body, divisible into certain well-defined departments, such as the head, lungs, heart, abdominal region, and so forth, these being sub-divisible into almost innumerable parts, composed of molecules and millions of minute "lives"; (2) of a reasoning faculty or mind, also heterogeneous in its nature, with countless contradictory elements, and thoughts which, collectively, might be compared to political parties in a state, seeing that they can be broadly classified in characteristic divisions; and (3), of an *ego*, or continuous sense of identity, sometimes called soul or spirit, with which the moral nature is frequently connected.

It will be readily seen that a nation is constituted in exactly the same way. A nation also owns property, incurs debts, buys and sells, has "social" relations with other states, is subject to the law of decay and death, its term of life being dependent upon the original soundness of its constitution, the conditions (hygienic or economic) in which it lives, and its escape from a sudden termination to its career as the result of accident by war, pestilence, or famine. It has moral and material obligations, as in the case of an individual.

The truth of this fundamental proposition, affirmed by so many philosophers,[1] is granted by the recognized authorities on international law,

[1] See Note A., on "A Nation an Organism."

who postulate "of those independent states which are dealt with by international law, that they have a moral nature identical with that of individuals, and that with respect to one another they are in the same relation as that in which individuals stand to each other who are subject to law. They are collective persons, and as such they have rights and are under obligations."[1]

It follows, therefore, that if we can determine with certainty, and with sufficient elasticity, what general principles ought to govern the relations of men with each other, we can, by means of an impregnable induction, determine what general principles ought to govern international relationships. But just as it would be unreasonable to expect the average individual to conduct his affairs wholly on the basis of right principle, so would it be to expect the same of a nation. Growth takes place gradually. After sudden impulse has more or less frequently led to right action, comes, in time, the recognition of right in itself. But the desire to do right and the ability to do so also take time to develop. Furthermore, there are certain departments of life in which it is easier to conform to principle than in others, because to do so requires less seeming sacrifice of personal interests, while

[1] *A Treatise on International Law*, Part I., chap. i., § 1, by W. E. Hall.

in many cases the benefits resulting from obedience to these laws are overwhelmingly manifest.

The first step, however, is to decide what principles *ought to be* conformed to; what, in other words, should be the *aim* of individuals and nations, not in the ultimate sense, but in the sense of the stage next to be reached. How this aim can be realized, and to what extent practical measures can be taken immediately to give preliminary effect to this recognition of principle, is another though equally important matter.

CHAPTER V.

Laws of Life.

THE past hundred years have witnessed an enormous development of the ethical idea among civilized people. The greatest thinkers and writers have devoted themselves to elucidating moral questions. Men and women of all creeds and philosophies have united in this work, so that it is no longer necessary to adopt a dogmatic attitude in propounding moral truths, even if that were still effective; and there is an element of native "cussedness" in most people, so that to say to them "Thou shalt not," is apt to incite the mental retort, "I shall."

The reasonableness of a rule of conduct must be made clear before it can be generally accepted by thinking people. The command, "Thou shalt not steal," for example, has been discussed from countless points of view, by Agnostics, Positivists, Materialists, Deists, Theists, Pantheists, Idealists, as well as by every known type of orthodox and heterodox Christian. All have adduced overwhelming arguments to prove that stealing is wrong. Some have claimed to be able to demonstrate logically that it is not only contrary to the moral law, but that it defeats its own end, if that end be the increase of personal happiness. From that point of view, and in other words, the crude truth is that stealing does not pay, while honesty does.

Certain authorities say that it is wise to be honest because it is right to be honest, approaching the matter from their ideal of right. Others say that it is right to be honest because it is wise to be honest, approaching the same question from the standpoint of experience.[1] From either point of view the result is the same; and this may be taken as additional proof that the truly ideal is also the truly practical, and that sound principle is "only another name for a proposition stating the terms" of a far-sighted instead of a short-sighted expediency.

There are extremists whom it annoys to be told that honesty pays. They look upon it as a degradation of the ideal, as a pandering to purely selfish instincts. "Avoid extremes," said Confucius, who generally showed good sense. Enlightened selfishness produces the same result, in action, as en-

[1] "There is much greater agreement among thoughtful persons on the question what a good life is, than on the question why it is good," says Professor Sidgwick in his *Practical Ethics* (p. 43).

lightened unselfishness—the enlightenment being the active partner in the combination.[1] That is the point that extremists overlook. They are of necessity lopsided and can never consider anything from more than one standpoint; they concern themselves with excrescences rather than with essences, and with superficialities instead of with fundamentals.

It is not even necessary to take the interdependence of humanity into account in order to show that hypocrisy, untruthfulness, malignity, hatred, injustice, covetousness, arrogance, cowardliness, ingratitude, improbity, intemperance, and all the vices are reactionary in their effect, tending to defeat instead of further their supposed ends.

A persistently untruthful man never deceives any one. A man imbued with hatred destroys his own happiness and almost invariably injures himself more than any one else. An intemperate man, if desirous of stimulating his consciousness, reaches a point at which he becomes oblivious of every sensation; while, if desirous of deadening his consciousness, he reaches a point at which its activity becomes agonizingly accentuated.

The law that every cause produces a proportionate effect and that every effect is preceded by some adequate cause, makes it impossible to sin against

[1] See Note B., on "Unselfishness."

nature without being punished by nature. Man must reap the seed of his own sowing, good, bad, and indifferent. Every force, once liberated, reacts back upon the centre from which it originated. Machiavelli's hero, Cæsar Borgia, was no exception to the rule—an object-lesson which seems to have been wasted upon the author of *Il Principe.*

"Foolish men imagine that because judgment for an evil thing is delayed, there is no justice, but an accidental one, here below. Judgment for an evil thing is many times delayed some day or two, some century or two, but it is sure as life, it is sure as death!" So spoke Carlyle, re-echoing the conclusions of every careful student of history, as of all those who have but observed the sequence of their own lives, irrespective of their religion, philosophy, or lack of either.

Just as the commission of positive wrong results in positive injury to the wrong-doer, so the active virtues bring with them their own reward. Take generosity, not only of purse, but of mind and sympathy. Is it not evident that the generous man—if he be truly generous, with the generosity that neither seeks nor expects compensation—arouses a like attitude toward himself in others? A generous employer will get far more work out of his men than could a niggard, and in a time of crisis his men would stand by him loyally, while they would seize their chance to make the niggard suffer for his treatment of them. To give generous measure is to bring generous returns in any trade.

Most truths are commonplace, ethical truths particularly. The difficulty, however, is to get them appreciated as being such, though the difficulty has been largely overcome where the everyday virtues are concerned. It is now generally conceded that to be temperate, honest, courageous, charitable, just, kindly, tolerant, truthful, and straightforward is not only right, but wise and even profitable. Let it be stated again that to do and to be otherwise is to court unnecessary suffering, for principles of right thought and action are truths of nature expressed in terms of ethics, and truths of nature are facts which cannot be gainsaid with comfort.

These active virtues may be classified as duties which man owes his fellows. If he does not try to fulfil them he is working against progress, against the great tide of universal life, and will consequently find himself overcome, if he live long enough, by the opposition he needlessly generates.

Such a statement may appear to impugn the theory of the struggle for existence and the resulting "survival of the fittest," but such an appearance would be totally delusive, for the statement is in direct accordance with the whole scheme of evolution. This was admirably demonstrated by Professor Huxley in his Romanes Lecture for 1893, on "Evolution and Ethics." In it he says:

"There is another fallacy which appears to me to pervade the so-called 'ethics of evolution.' It is the notion that because, on the whole, animals and plants have advanced in perfection of organization by means of the struggle for existence and the consequent 'survival of the fittest'; therefore men in society, men as ethical beings, must look to the same process to help them towards perfection. I suspect that this fallacy has arisen out of the unfortunate ambiguity of the phrase 'survival of the fittest.' 'Fittest' has a connotation of 'best'; and about 'best' there hangs a moral flavour. In cosmic nature, however, *what is 'fittest' depends upon the conditions.* . . .

"Men in society are undoubtedly subject to the cosmic process. As among other animals, multiplication goes on without cessation and involves severe competition for the means of support. The struggle for existence tends to eliminate those less fitted to adapt themselves to the circumstances of their existence. The strongest, the most self-assertive, tend to tread down the weaker. But the influence of the cosmic process on the evolution of society is the greater the more rudimentary its civilization. Social progress means a checking of the cosmic process at every step and the substitution for it of another, which may be called the ethical process; the end of which is not the survival of those who may happen to be the fittest, in respect of the whole of the conditions which exist, but of those who are ethically the best."

In a note Professor Huxley explains that "Of course, strictly speaking, social life and the ethical process in virtue of which it advances towards perfection, are part and parcel of the general process of evolution."[1]

Humanity is interdependent, like the solar system, in which each planet revolves upon its own axis, yet is affected by the other planets, all of which are dependent upon each other and the centralizing sun for their positions, movements, and very existence.

Circulation is a *sine qua non* of life; isolation results in death. No man can cut himself off from the community in which he lives. He is a vital part of it, and as a part he owes to other parts certain duties, many of which are ethical; and if he does not fulfil these and so share in the circulation of the organic body in which he is incorporated, he

---

[1] *Evolution and Ethics*, pp. 32, 33 and Note 19. For Mr. Herbert Spencer's views on the same subject, see Note C., in this volume, on "The Morality of the Evolutionary Process."

dies—ethically, in any event—after having undergone innumerable injuries and pains, moral, mental, and material, just as a limb or an organ dies if it does not perform its part in the human system.

Those who perpetually proclaim the rights of the individual as an independent entity are extremists after their kind; those who over-insist upon the paramount rights of society over the individual are extremists after theirs. Both place the individual in opposition to his fellows. There is "the middle path," which, being the path of nature and of fact, reconciles the two extremes. And that is the path of duty: not the everlasting assertion of rights, but the fulfilment of duty—that is the road to prosperity and progress, and that places the individual, not in opposition to his fellows, but in accord with them, dependent upon them as they are dependent upon him.[1]

There is the duty of the individual (a) to himself, (b) to other individuals, (c) to the community of which he is a part, and (d) to other communities (nations). Until he recognizes these duties to

---

[1] "The things that people stand most in need of being reminded of are, one would think, their duties—for their rights, whatever they may be, they are apt enough to attend to of themselves."—Jeremy Bentham's "Works," vol. ii., p. 51. It is hardly to be supposed that Bentham's utilitarianism can be considered sentimental, even by the most "practical" of politicians.

some extent and at least tries to fulfil them, he can hardly be said to have touched the sphere of civilization. He is not even selfish in the enlightened sense, for, as has been said already, enlightened selfishness produces the same results, *in action*, as enlightened unselfishness.

It would not be profitable to attempt to discriminate between the duties man owes himself and those he owes his fellows. His doing of both right and of wrong reacts upon himself, while others are affected by it both directly and indirectly: directly as the result of the action, and indirectly as the result of example. Just, he upholds the ideal of justice; law-abiding, he inspires respect for law and order; self-reliant and considerate of the rights of others, he stands as a representative of liberty. His responsibility in this respect is a serious one, and the more prominent his position among men, the greater must be his responsibility.

These, broadly speaking, are the conclusions which most thinking people have arrived at, concerning the principles of conduct which should govern the relations of individuals with each other.

CHAPTER VI.

Principles of National Conduct.

It was shown in the first place that every one is in some way concerned in international affairs; that no one can remain unaffected by the doings of his own country in relation to others, nor even by complications between states on the other side of the globe.

It was then shown that it would be advisable for every one not only to seek to discover the laws which govern this department of universal life and the principles upon which action connected therewith should be based, but to stand immovably by such principles, once discovered, refusing—so far as possible—to be influenced by merely ephemeral considerations, taking the wider instead of the narrow view, thinking of years and the harvest of years as well as of the showing of days and of hours.

Following this, it was pointed out that to understand the laws governing the physical, mental, and moral development of an individual is to understand the laws governing the physical, mental, and moral development of a nation; that to determine

PRINCIPLES OF NATIONAL CONDUCT. 53

the general principles which should govern the relations of men with each other is to determine the general principles which should govern international relationships.

Lastly, the principles of conduct which should govern the relations of individuals with each other were reviewed, and from what was then said it must follow that a nation—supposing it claims to have passed the wild-beast stage of its evolution—must have duties to perform similar to those which should be binding upon men; that it too *should* stand as a representative of liberty, of law and order; that it too *should* uphold the ideal of justice. It may not always succeed, but the effort should be made. Failing in this, it fails to attempt the performance of its duty; continually failing to perform its various duties (*a*) to itself, (*b*) to other nations, and (*c*) to the world as a whole, it will sooner or later come to a standstill in its development, stagnate, and then die. By violating principle it invites disaster, and nature steps in to put an end to one of her products that has ceased to perform its function. By refusing to recognize the "ethical process" (using Professor Huxley's terminology), and by adhering to the material or "cosmic process" *after that has ceased to be the means of growth*, a nation moves against the current of universal life, every movement giving rise to friction both within and without itself as it retrogresses and disintegrates.

The greater a nation's strength and attainments as a result of the cosmic process, the more urgent the need for it to adapt itself to the conditions which the social state introduces. Having reached the acme of brute development, its decline will be all the more swift unless it conforms to the requirements of nature, submits to the ethical process, and adopts the social habits.

Instead of ceaselessly proclaiming its rights, with a jealousy that would be ridiculous in an individual, it must pay at least some attention to its duties, for only in that way can it survive the struggle for existence, the result of which is, after a certain point, the survival of "those who are ethically the best."

But for a nation suddenly to change its policy would be almost undesirable, even supposing it were possible. Sudden "conversions" are too frequently followed by sudden submersions, in more senses than one. Extremes are always wrong. Nature never hurries in her processes. Mental and moral evolution, to be healthy, must take place by the extension of previous ideas and the accentuation of previously existing tendencies. Yet, if we see the first small sprouting from an acorn, the promise of a future oak-tree is before

PRINCIPLES OF NATIONAL CONDUCT. 55

our eyes; and if it be possible to detect the faintest ethical tendency in the conduct of one or more nations at the present time, we may be sure that this tendency is the promise of the moral development in question.

Although, broadly speaking, in the case of man, the same ethical conceptions and rules of conduct have been promulgated by the world's greatest teachers in every historical period, the capacity of the average individual to appreciate ethics has not remained the same. In the course of his evolution from a barbarous to a civilized condition, it is evident that his conception of right and wrong has undergone considerable alteration. The moral standard of the nineteenth-century Briton, for instance, is in many respects a good deal higher than that of his progenitor as portrayed by Julius Cæsar.[1]

National morality must be subject to the same law; it, too, must change; and though no hasty

[1] It is probable that in a thousand years from now our present standard of morality will be considered primitive in the extreme; but this need not necessarily involve the supposition that right and wrong change in themselves. All that it proves is that man's power to discriminate between the two is a faculty that develops in the course of time as the result of his increasing experience. His moral responsibility must be proportionate to his ability to discriminate between good and evil, and on this account there is truth in the saying that what is right in one age is wrong in another.

change is to be looked for or desired, it must be fatal to the welfare of a state to be hide-bound by precedent. Conditions vary, and conduct must keep pace with the conditions of progress.

While many nations have taken the first step in their ethical development by the unpremeditated doing of right, few, if any, have taken the second—the recognition of right principle or general law upon which their conduct should be based. A narrow policy has been their only guide, redeemed at times by outbursts of noble sentiment and generous impulse. Sentiment, however, is notoriously unreliable as a motive power; its direction is always uncertain, and although it may occasionally conduce to good, its results are frequently evil. Just men have been burned at the stake on sentimental grounds. Recognition of general laws is necessary before a consistent and consecutive course of action can be followed, and nations, to progress, must endeavour to conform to them.

No matter how long it may take, the present ethical ideal of man must, in the course of evolution, become the ethical ideal of nations; and the longer this is deferred the longer will suffering continue, resulting from the violation of right principle.

The higher the aim the higher will be the attainment; but although it would be almost hopeless to set up as an immediate and practical aim the fulfilment by nations of all their duties, there are undoubtedly certain duties which, already recognized to some extent, need to be more widely appreciated, and the tendency to fulfil them accentuated by every means possible.

It was discovered long ago, and has often been pointed out, that a vanquished state reaps the benefit of an honourable reputation, for if its promises cannot be relied upon by the victor, self-interest will impel the victor to annihilate the victim. More recently it has been dawning upon the international consciousness that to be truthful, honest, just, conciliatory, tolerant, and even generous, is not only right, but actually profitable. This most desirable state of things is attributable to the growing perception that nations, like individuals, are interdependent; that their interests are fundamentally the same; that what injures one injures all, and that the welfare of one reacts advantageously upon the rest.

The consistent application of this principle is vigorously and even bitterly opposed by some people, who, shameless where the alleged welfare of their country is concerned, clamour for "practical" procedure, publicly defining this as a policy whose aim it is to get as much and to give as little as possible, quite regardless of the consequences to other nations—and quite regardless of consequences to their own, if they had sense enough to see it.[1]

Much is it to be regretted that these benighted individuals, who perpetually plume themselves upon being worldly-wise, and who denounce any reference to principle as sentimental, do not pause to discover what a principle is. The subject has been admirably elucidated by thinkers and writers who have never been accused of either sanctimony or romanticism.

The person who announces himself as practical would hardly deny that in the commercial world experience has fully demonstrated that, in the long run, a firm with a reputation for unimpeachable honesty has an enormous advantage over its competitors; he would probably claim, if he were English, that one explanation of England's "supremacy in trade" is that its manufacturers have the reputation of actually selling what they promise to sell; he might go so far as to confess that a politician who keeps his word and who gives evidence of love of country rather than of love of self, and of fairness in dealing with his opponents, is more likely to succeed in the end than one who will do and say anything to catch a vote or to gain a temporary advantage over his political adversaries. But the

[1] See Note D., on "'Splendid Isolation,' or the Interdependence of Nations."

same person protests against the application of such principles in foreign affairs, not content with the *quid pro quo* which he adopts as his shibboleth, and insisting that a policy of "expansive acquisition" is the only sensible course to pursue—an international kleptomaniac, judged charitably. He perhaps forgets that "each for himself and the devil take the hindmost," inevitably results in the devil taking the lot.

But this brazen contempt for ethics is a mere relic of the brute struggle for existence at any price, and those who favour it are the reversions, unavoidable in evolution. The long-lost stripes of the wild horse will appear occasionally in the present domesticated animal.

There are others, however, who feel themselves obliged to countenance dishonesty in international procedure, and who do so with regret. Their intentions are good.

These modern apologists for Machiavellianism urge that as other countries do things they ought not to do, their own must follow suit in order to protect itself; that is to say, if you are so unfortunate as to live among robbers, you too must rob or—"get left." Waiving the indisputable immorality of such conduct, has not experience proved that it is the negatively good man who suffers?—the man whom it rather grieves to do evil and who yet tries to imitate unscrupulous associates so as to keep level with them, possibly in the hope of outreaching them while preserving his own morality. It was to him that the "voice as the sound of many waters" said, "Because thou art lukewarm, and neither cold nor hot, I will spue thee out of my mouth."

Ask the average person, If you lived among robbers, would you rob? Merely because you saw robbery going on around you, would it be reasonable to suppose that all men were not only robbers, but that they all *wanted* to be robbers? Would not a bold declaration of principles on your part, and strict adherence to those principles by you, so greatly astonish some of your neighbours as to shock or inspire them into following your example? Would you not in any case gather around yourself those who did not want to rob, and in this way change the character of the community from "all goats" into "goats and some sheep"? The average person knows that if you cannot at once transform, you may leaven. How, otherwise, is progress possible?

Ask a nation if it would join in the spoliation of a friendly power because a combination of other powers threatened to treat it in the same way if it refused to further the transaction. There are but few countries that would not resent such a proposal, preferring to take the consequences of refusal, whatever they might be.

Of course, if a nation is constitutionally and incurably dishonest, and does not pretend to be anything else, it can only follow a career of scoundrelism, and may meet with considerable success for a time, though its end is sure. It would be difficult, however, to imagine a nation deliberately classifying itself under this head; and if there are still some countries, behind the rest in civilization, where Machiavellianism receives the *cachet* of the Government, it can no longer be regarded as the religion of the multitude.

CHAPTER VII.

THE PROMISE OF RECENT PRACTICE.

THE better practice of the more civilized communities already speaks for itself, containing the promise of a high moral development in the future, based upon the principle of interdependence.

The practice of the United Kingdom, for example, may not have been undeviating; her Governments may not always have supported her claim; but that claim has been that she stands among nations as an upholder of justice and freedom, as a protector of the down-trodden and oppressed, and as

> "A safeguard, a sheltering land,
> In the thunder and torrent of years."

This claim, irrespective of practice, is a tacit recognition of the duties in question, even if the principle of interdependence, upon which these duties are based, has only been appreciated by the thinking minority. Nor can the practice be condemned as wholly unworthy of the claim, for Great Britain has shown herself capable of being swayed by magnificent emotions and of doing most generous deeds.

It was she who first abolished the Slave Trade, afterward liberating the slaves in her colonies and dependencies, compensating their owners for the loss. It was she who gave right of asylum in the face of an almost united Europe. Ever since 1824 she has done her utmost to help the cause of Greek independence, in spite of its having been her "policy" to save the Ottoman Empire from disintegration. Belgium could hardly have secured her independence without Great Britain's help. In Spain and Portugal constitutional government found in her its warmest supporter as against the absolutism of the "Holy Alliance." Her sympathy with the Italian provinces in their efforts to regain their freedom and form a united country will not soon be forgotten by Italy. The cause of Hungary aroused the greatest enthusiasm, and all political parties combined to welcome Kossuth. Great Britain admittedly regretted not having persisted in her intervention on behalf of the Poles in 1863; and, rightly or wrongly, the indignation of her people knew no bounds at the inaction of the Government in failing to support Denmark in the following year. The massacres by the Druses at Beyrout and Damascus resulted in her active intervention. Rarely has such a storm of indignation been aroused in any country as that evoked in Great Britain by the Bulgarian atrocities of 1875 and 1876. Her more recent action in regard to Armenia and Crete, much criticised as it has been, particularly by her own people, was at least an attempt to pursue the same generous course. Her attitude in the Cuban question was by no means entirely based upon her friendship for the United States, for no British Government would dare take action against any people struggling for their freedom, once they were known to be oppressed. The great mass of her population would ignore every question of policy in dealing with a matter of that sort.

Over and over again Great Britain has made it her business to see that justice was done, that freedom was upheld, that the oppressed were protected, that order was maintained, that constitutionalism was recognized. She has committed herself beyond any question to the principle of interdependence, admitting that what injured another injured her and all others, and that she had duties to perform even before she had rights to sustain.

If the United States of America has made fewer assertions in this respect than Great Britain, and if the necessities of internal development have absorbed her attention until recently, she has nevertheless shown the same spirit and has made considerable sacrifices in order to do what she conceived to be her duty in relation to the welfare of others. Whatever may be said by hostile critics in regard to her war with Spain—that it was a politicians' war, and so forth—those who know the facts know that it was the people of the United States who insisted upon its being waged, and that they did this, not from any selfish motive such as the acquisition of Cuba, but because of their profound sympathy for the insurgents and because of their horror and indignation at the reports which reached them of the treatment to which the *reconcentrados* were subjected by the Spanish officials.

"When the modern friends of Spain in the United States jeeringly ask why we should trouble ourselves about the Cubans or Armenians or Cretans, and go so far afield with our sympathies, they fail to remember the history of their own country. They forget the Congress which, stirred by the splendor of Webster's eloquence, sent words of encouragement to the Greeks. They forget whose sympathies went far across the waters to the Hungarians, and who were the people who brought Kossuth to safety in one of their own men-of-war. . . . Sympathy for men fighting for freedom anywhere is distinctively American, and when from fear or greed or from absorption in merely material things we despise and abandon it, we shall not only deny our history and our birthright, but our faith in our own Republic, and all we most cherish will fade and grow dim."[1]

The United Kingdom of Great Britain and Ireland and the United States of America by no means stand alone in their practical recognition of the duties arising from the interdependence of nations; and so general has this recognition become, on the part of the civilized Powers, that international law, based according to most of its exponents upon custom only, takes full cognizance of these duties and devotes much attention to their definition.

It has been shown already that it is postulated by Hall and other writers that independent states have a "moral nature," and as such are "under obligations" and have duties to perform. The individual," says Bluntschli, "does not completely satisfy the call of moral duty if he merely does what is right within his own sphere of activity, without offering a hand to others who need it to do right in their sphere: and just as little does a state entirely fulfil its task if it acts justly in its own dominions, but declines to give to other states the help of which they are in want."[2]

---

[1] *Certain Accepted Heroes and Other Essays*, by Henry Cabot Lodge (Republican Senator from Massachusetts); art., "Our Foreign Policy." The views on the same subject of Mr. Richard Olney, Democratic Secretary of State during Mr. Cleveland's second administration, will be found in Note D.

[2] *Staatswörterbuch*, i, 501, quoted by Hall.

THE PROMISE OF RECENT PRACTICE. 67

Interdependence is again admitted in the rule that a "treaty is not binding which has for its object the subjugation or partition of a country, unless the existence of the latter is wholly incompatible with the general security; and an agreement for the assertion of proprietary rights over the open ocean would be invalid, because the freedom of the open seas from appropriation, though an arbitrary principle, is one that is fully received into international law.... A compact for the establishment of a slave trade would be void, because the personal freedom of human beings has been admitted by modern civilized states as a right which they are bound to respect and which they ought to uphold internationally."[1]

"Merely the opening of water-ways now renders intercourse among the nations practically unavoidable; and civilized or uncivilized, willingly or unwillingly, they will all have to enter into more or less close relations with one another. Just how close those relations should be, international law does not prescribe, for it is reluctant to derogate from the privileges of sovereignty. It does, however, enjoin on the nations the duties of comity and humanity, and when they enter into closer relations it provides rules to be observed not only in establishing them, but in maintaining them, or in

[1] *A Treatise on International Law*, by W. E. Hall, § 108.

breaking them off. Specific rules it does not furnish to meet every case; but, when they are wanting, it has general rules that apply, including those that recommend justice and morality." [1]

That a diplomatic agent "should exert his influence during a period of war or of grave disorder to protect the citizens or subjects of friendly nations and their property"; that he may "interpose his good offices even in behalf of natives of the country in which he acts, if they are threatened with, or subjected to, treatment inconsistent with the principles of humanity"; that "a nation may refuse to be bound by a treaty stipulating that it should perform an unlawful or immoral or a criminal act, and other nations may interfere to prevent it from being committed or may properly protest against it if it has already been committed"; that a nation may mediate to prevent war, may intervene to "suppress crime of governments against their peoples, or to stop a nefarious action on the part of a strong power against a weaker one," [2] or for other cause—all proves that nations have moral duties to perform toward each other, that they recognize the fact, and that in so doing they recognize the fundamental principle of interdependence.

[1] *International Law*, by H. W. Bowen, § 33.
[2] Bowen, §§ 62, 109, 120, 219.

CHAPTER VIII.

THE LESSONS OF THE CENTURIES.

THE recognition of international duties has been rapidly increasing during the present century. It would almost seem that every century has its distinct lesson for the leading nations of the world, and that these lessons are progressive, as it were, originating in the minds of men, often in modifications of their religious beliefs, and then finding expression in the internal affairs of states, finally in international affairs. The appreciation of individual and national Rights came about in this way: first, in the proclamation that man had the inalienable right to think for himself in religious matters—in other words, that he had the right to govern his own mind. As a logical application of this principle came the declaration that communities had the right to govern themselves; and only as people came to accept the first lesson did they accept and insist upon the second. Finally, the same principle was applied internationally, and for long the Rights of Nations absorbed the attention of the civilized world—were fought for, just as men had fought for their individual and collective rights.

Between each stage in the progressive march of the idea, between each wider application of the principle, came reactionary stages, so that progress was frequently interrupted, the general advance being comparable to a rising tide, its steady forward movement being sometimes lost sight of in the backward and forward wash of its waves. Thus the American Colonies were opposed to the English Government on the same grounds, roughly speaking, as those on which the people of England opposed the unfortunate King Charles; but in the second event it took a very short time for the fact to be recognized that the American Colonies had been perfectly right in their stand.

At the very time that the Rights of Nations were being most vigorously asserted, another and more inspiring idea was being proclaimed by men of every sect as of no sect. This was the recognition of the *Duties* man owes to himself and his fellows as being of more importance than a mere insistance upon his *Rights*. On all sides, in every department of life, it came to be seen by many that a full and faithful performance by individuals of these duties would solve more of the world's problems than a perpetual claiming of prerogatives. The idea began to influence governments in their attitude toward the governed, and the next expression taken by this great conception of duty was legislative;—Factory Acts, Usury Acts, and every conceivable sort of an Act designed to protect and promote the well-being of rich and poor alike, followed each other in quick succession.

Side by side with this development, the same principle came to be applied in international matters, not only by Great Britain and by the United States, but by all the more highly civilized nations, until the elementary duties they owe to each other have been defined in treaties and have been incorporated in statements of international custom. And while individuals at first, and then nations, formerly co-operated in order to enforce their Rights, individuals have now learned to co-operate in order to fulfil their Duties, the last extension of the idea being the co-operation of nations for the same ennobling object—interdependence enlarging the outlook of independence and saving it from the mad extreme of isolation.

Not for self only, but with due regard for the welfare of others: nothing lower than this can be a worthy aim for a civilized community. Such an aim would not merely enable it to keep pace with the "ethical process" in evolution, but would give its deeds a loftiness of purpose and a power that the policies of the past have failed to give them.

Writing in 1852, Mazzini said that "since 1815 there has been a great want in Europe—the *initiative* has disappeared; it belongs to no country at the present time. . . . Europe is in search of it; no one knows yet by which people it will be seized."[1]

That initiative is still lacking, for although the last century produced more than one Declaration of Rights (as Mazzini observed), this century has not yet produced a Declaration of Principles; and until such a declaration of principles is formulated, and so long as the prevailing recognition of certain duties, satisfactory though it is, remains as vague and casual as at present, it can fall to the lot of no nation to seize the initiative and become the leader of the world's advance.

Rapid strides have been made, however, since 1852. In the womb of Nature many things are hidden, awaiting the hour of their deliverance, gaining strength, unseen, in the darkness, that they may be strong in the light. And in the womb of the world's experience has been growing a possession beyond all price—the new inspiration for the birth of which the nations have long been waiting. But like a woman, waiting for the birth of her first-born, not realizing as yet what a blessing she carries with her, bringing as it will a new initiative into her life, a new hope into her heart, so

[1] *Essays*, "Europe: Its Condition," by Joseph Mazzini.

the nations have not yet grasped the full significance of this that waits within them for expression, giving them as it will, a new aspiration, a new aim for their existence, a new and much-needed impetus.

A clear declaration of principles by one or more nations, and a single practical application of these principles to existing difficulties—and the international lesson of the nineteenth century will have been learned, the work of the twentieth begun.[1]

[1] See Note E., on "Christianity."

Part Third.
PARTICULAR CONSIDERATIONS.

CHAPTER IX.

A TEST OF PROGRESS.

ONCE the interdependence of nations is recognized, and it is seen that injury to one involves injury to others, that the welfare of one affects others beneficially, and that they owe each other duties as well as having rights, it only remains to decide what should be the first positive, practical application of these principles internationally, as a logical continuation of the tentative applications already made.

It has been shown in a previous chapter that the growth of nations is governed by the same laws that govern the growth of individuals, and that a nation and an individual follow the same path in their development. Consequently, in order to discover this next practical step — to be taken consciously, let us hope, with a full understanding of the principle or law upon which it is based — it will be necessary to follow the stages by which men have come to express in concerted action, slowly but surely and as the result of increasing experience, their appreciation of the interdependence of a community of individuals, of the duties they owe to each other, and of their underlying unity of interest. Having arrived at this process, the results can be compared with what is known of the lives of nations, and it can then be decided whether nations are as far advanced in practice as individuals, and if not, what is the next step to be taken in their development.

It has been suggested already that man's increasing sense of responsibility to his fellows has found expression in legislation, based upon the principle of interdependence. For many years past the great legal doctrine has been universally accepted, that *a wrong done to any member of the community is a wrong done to the community itself*, and so to the king or governing power as its head. This doctrine has more recently been interpreted so as to include the idea that what benefits the individual benefits the state—the positive application of the negative rule. Hence, legislation has been much concerned, not only with the protection of all classes, but with the improvement of the conditions in which they live and labour, with their education, health, and so forth.

It is said to be the object of law to "define and protect the rights of persons and to defend .the individual liberties of all"—a sufficiently comprehensive and elastic statement of its aims, for so much depends upon the definition of a person's "rights." One hundred years ago it would never have been admitted that a factory hand had a right to work in sanitary conditions, or that it was the duty of a government to see that such conditions were provided. Only when it came to be seen that it would benefit the nation as a whole if he were protected in this way, and that he had a moral right to the protection, was this right embodied in law; for it is the aim of law to make, so far as it can, a moral right a legal right.

In the same way it is the aim of law to make a moral duty a legal duty, which would naturally follow from the fact that wherever one person has a right, another has a duty in relation to that person. Thus, if a wife has a right to the support of her husband, it is the duty of her husband to support her; if a factory hand has a right to work in sanitary conditions, his employer has the duty of providing them.

Such considerations make it abundantly evident that the laws of a nation at any one time are a faithful representation of its collective moral sense and of its appreciation of general laws, though here, as elsewhere, action follows thought, and it takes time for action to modify form. Growth of the moral perceptions, however, invariably produces a corresponding development in the laws of the land, this being true, not only of self-governing communities, but of nations governed despotically, as of nations controlled by custom and precedent whether embodied in laws or not. In every case, any improvement in the general sense of justice, of responsibility, any increase in the general understanding of interdependence, is certain to result in a corresponding change in the prevailing laws.

"Our human laws," said Froude, "are but the copies, more or less imperfect, of the eternal laws, so far as we can read them." And as fast as men read the eternal laws of nature, as their understanding of utility broadens, and as they perceive more and more clearly that the truly moral is the truly useful, and *vice versa*, they give expression, in the form of law, to their mental and moral growth. It would be as unwise for them not to do this as it would be unwise for them deliberately to violate any other law of nature, once they recognize its existence.

Individuals, acting collectively through their representatives, legislate for their mutual protection and for the general benefit of the community. Nations do not legislate in their collective capacity, and it would therefore seem that nations are debarred from expressing their growing recognition of interdependence in the same way as individuals. But it should be remembered that it is only within comparatively recent times that individuals have had legislative power. They, of their own volition, could not always give direct legal expression to their moral perceptions. Representative government is a modern development, and it took centuries for law to become what it now is.

Although nations do not legislate as among themselves, what is called "International Law" is a recognized factor in governing the relations of states. It is therefore important to determine in what respects International Law corresponds to municipal or state law.

According to Hall, it is comparable in many respects with the condition of the law "when the early Teutonic societies allowed a person, upon whom a certain kind of legal injury had been inflicted, to seize the cattle of the wrong-doer and keep them till he obtained satisfaction, or when they told him to refer a quarrel involving legal questions to the issue of trial by combat. . . ." International Law is like the state law of that early period inasmuch as it has not been enacted and merely consists of a record of precedents, sometimes good and sometimes bad, which are followed in much the same way as precedents in social etiquette are followed. The term "law" is an entire misnomer for such a code, for no country can be said to be governed by law unless means are provided for its enforcement. Individuals sometimes use force to punish a breach of etiquette, but procedure of that kind can hardly be dignified by comparison with judicial methods. Early Teutonic law was occasionally enforced in much the same way: like modern International Law, it consisted largely of rules regulating trial by combat, ultimately classified by some contemporary Marquis of Queensberry, with stipulations in regard to the correct behaviour of neutral bystanders. Hardly a satisfactory state of affairs.

If this be conceded, and if it be further conceded that the moral and utilitarian perceptions of the individuals composing the civilized nations are no longer represented fairly by laws of that order, it will be well to determine (a) how the Teutonic laws originated, and (b) through what stages they passed before reaching the high standard of our present legal systems; for just as the growth of nations is governed by the same natural laws as those governing the growth of individuals, so international law must have been derived in the same way as state law, and its development, in the past as in the future, must be subject to the same general laws as those controlling the growth of state law. In this way it will be possible to determine

A TEST OF PROGRESS.

the next step that international law should take in its evolution—that it *must* take, seeing that evolution is universal in nature, and seeing also that in this case the process of growth of an exactly similar thing is known already.

It is strange that while millions of people in all parts of the world have been deeply interested for years in the development of state law, every act of a state legislature being narrowly watched, only a small proportion of that number have shown interest in the condition of international law until quite lately. Every one would admit that for a man to care nothing for laws involving his country as a whole, while deeply concerning himself in the administration of his own city, would be strong evidence of his narrow-mindedness. The larger laws affect him quite as much as those obtaining locally. Yet those who take an interest in the law and legislation of their own nation, and who yet know nothing and care as little for the larger international law, are equally narrow in their outlook. Fortunately, this too is coming to be generally admitted.

CHAPTER X.

THE EVOLUTION OF STATE LAW.

THE actual origin of law is a moot point, though the later stages of its evolution have been very clearly established. Most modern authorities on the subject begin by postulating the existence of primitive man, whom they proceed to endow with certain characteristics. But the trouble is that no one knows anything about him, and to dogmatize about a postulate is certainly foolish. Most of the savage races of to-day are at least as likely to be degenerate survivals of otherwise extinct races, as to be primitive people on the ascendant arc of evolution. As far back as history has anything to report, it tells of high civilization, in Central and Southern America, in Asia and elsewhere. Hence there is need for caution in accepting hypothetical explanations of the genesis of legal and similar institutions. It should not be forgotten that according to the theory of evolution, as expounded by Herbert Spencer, Professor Huxley, and others, as also according to its earlier Greek and Hindu exponents, "evolution must reach a limit, after which a reverse change must begin," involution or absorption following evolution, and evolution, involution; these processes following each other alternately.

So it is not easy to deal with the origin of law in an entirely orthodox manner. Any view concerning it must remain hypothetical, owing to the uncertainty regarding man's primitive condition. Nor is it by any means a vital point in connection with the present inquiry, which is dependent only upon the later and well-ascertained stages in the evolution of human law. One may speculate usefully, and this is the speculation generally indulged in:

Taking the savage of to-day as a clue to the character of primitive man, it is seen that between him and civilized man there is a very considerable gulf where action is concerned, though both are subject to much the same loves and hates, jealousies and ambitions, hopes and fears. When the uncivilized man has a quarrel with his neighbour he adopts the handy but barbaric expedient of hitting him over the head with a club, and so puts an end to the quarrel by putting an end to the neighbour. He may go so far as to include his neighbour's wife and family in what he deems a necessary removal of impediments; and this, from that point of view, is often judicious, if immoral, for the reason that a desire for revenge comes naturally to uncivilized man, and the biter is apt to be badly bitten in his turn.

Whatever may be the desires of civilized man, he does not usually hit his neighbour over the head when he quarrels with him, because, among other and possibly better reasons, he knows that such a proceeding would seriously endanger his own life. Even supposing that other neighbours do not step in to prevent such a summary disposal of the case, the minions of the law, whom he helps to support by the payment of taxes, would almost inevitably bring him to justice. So he is likely to settle his dispute by a voluntary appeal to the law in the first place, instead of allowing the law to settle him, irrespective of his own volition.

This more peaceful method of procedure has resulted from a very long experience, in the course of which it was learned that a breach of the peace by two people was more than likely to lead to a breach of the peace by many, and that, apart from the sanctity of human life which also came to be admitted, it was for the best interest of all concerned to insist upon the preservation of order, even at some sacrifice of personal liberty of action, by the enactment of laws, mutually agreed upon or formulated by rulers, and by the appointment of guardians of the law to see that it was properly administered and enforced. But centuries passed before this conclusion was reached.

First—following the generally accepted theory— as uncivilized man was brought into closer touch with his fellows, brawls became more frequent, and the lives of others being consequently endangered, bystanders, objecting to their own promiscuous slaughter, supported some tribal priest or chieftain in forcible interference, who, while sometimes dispensing justice, would almost as frequently confine himself to giving a decision. Thus, if the possession of some animal, killed in the chase, were in dispute, one disputant was liable to get the head and the other the tail, while the arbiter took the rest: perhaps as his commission. This apparently unjust verdict might well have been defended on the ground that if either disputant got the trunk, the other would reject the decision and would revert to his club to see that justice was done; hence, from that point of view, it became the positive duty of the priest or chieftain to see that neither disputant got anything worth having. Still, there were of course exceptions to the rule, and equitable decisions must have been given deliberately as well as accidentally. Priests and chieftains were probably not accustomed to exercise much discrimination in regard to facts, and as there were no laws and at first very few customs to go by, they could only do their best and take the consequences.

Forcible intervention did not by any means put an end to fighting between individuals. In the course of time, however, a rough sense of honour was developed, putting some restraint upon combatants, and obliging them to give notice of their intention to fight. As the appreciation of right gradually improved, and as experience proved that fair play was desirable and benefited all parties, certain positive rules were evolved, such as the early rules of Chivalry and Knighthood, regulating combats, and, though unwritten, were well defined and widely observed among the better class of the community.

Meanwhile forcible intervention still continued, capricious and irresponsible as it must often have been, whether undertaken by king, chieftain, or priest. For these various stages overlap each other, and while that which constitutes one stage is developing still higher modes of expression, the germs of the next stage already exist and are rapidly gaining strength. Early types invariably persist after new ones appear. Modern duelling is an example of this law.

As time passed, custom in regard to the tenure of land and similar matters became more clearly defined. The decisions of former chieftains, re-

THE EVOLUTION OF STATE LAW. 89

vered as having been just men, or of priests whose holiness and learning had become proverbial, formed a constantly growing body of precedent, influencing decisions, and, in the case of minor disputes, making fresh decisions unnecessary, as the parties at issue would avoid the spoliation so likely to result from intervention, by voluntarily accepting these earlier judgments as applicable to the matter in dispute.

In consequence of the increasing population and as the governing power became more centralized, owing to conquests and other causes, this governing power found it necessary to appoint umpires to settle disputes. Men came to have a money value, and instead of allowing an injured person or his friends to take private vengeance for the injury, on the principle of "an eye for an eye and a tooth for a tooth," the umpires would fix upon a sum of money as compensation for the injury, even if the injury had proved mortal, in which case the compensation had to be paid to the family. This was the unwritten rule in Homeric Greece as in Teutonic England.

Only after the conversion of England to Christianity was the right to bequeath property recognized, and at about the same time joint or corporate ownership was introduced. Following this, and as another result of the introduction of

Christianity, came the system of direct appeal to the judgment of God by means of "ordeals."

Then, still considering the evolution of English law, came the first definite formulation of laws in writing, by Œthelberht, Offa, Ine, later by Ælfred, Æthelston, and Eadmund. These were based entirely on custom, but the system of mutual responsibility was enlarged. William the Conqueror modified these laws, as, for instance, in the appeal to the judgment of God, the English ordeal and the Norman wager of battle being alike legalized and regulated. But these modifications were mere amplifications of previously existing customs.

The present system of English law may be said to have taken its rise in the reign of Henry II. Even then, law remained a simple statement or confirmation of custom. Original law-making, in England, was a much later development, and did not really occur until, based upon the Saxon notion of crime as injury to the commonwealth, the great legal doctrine came to be formally accepted, that a wrong done to any member of the community is a wrong done to the community itself, and so to the king or governing power as its head. By that time principles of law had been sought and found, and precedent ceased to be the only basis for legal enactments and decisions. By that time, too, the establishment of laws was no longer the exclusive

THE EVOLUTION OF STATE LAW. 91

right of kings: the people, or a proportion of the people, represented in assembly, enacted laws, which were at most confirmed by the king.

Until then, laws had been forced upon people by the dominant power, whether they liked it or not, on a basis of arbitrary intervention. From that time on, the nation became more and more autonomous, though it can hardly be said that the people of England made their own laws and deliberately agreed to conform to them until the Reform Bill of 1832 had been passed. The famous Parliament of 1265 was in no sense a representative assembly. Its members were not elected: they were selected and summoned to attend by De Montfort.

Throughout the earlier part of this development, and till the stage last referred to had been reached, there had been in a very real sense "one law for the weak and another for the strong." The Barons of England, for instance, under the feudal system, had never considered themselves bound by the same laws that governed their dependents. They refused to concede their right of private vengeance to any one. Such a concession would have seemed like a surrender of their liberty of action, which they cherished as men, but more particularly as Barons. The consequence of this was a continuation by them of the old trial by combat; and as that led to bloody feuds, involving large numbers of retainers, disturbing the general peace and the welfare of the country as a whole, so strong a feeling was aroused against the practice, both on the part of king and people, that the Barons were at last compelled to adopt some other expedient in order to settle their differences.

Many of them had come to realize that these internecine feuds, often taking place as they did between members of the same family, were radically wrong, being contrary to the moral law as well as running counter to their own best interests. But rather than submit their differences to the ordinary courts, or even to adjudication by their peers, which still seemed to them to involve a surrender of their liberty of action as well as of their dignity, they frequently agreed upon an arbitrator, voluntarily submitting the matter in dispute to him, sometimes accepting and sometimes rejecting his decision. The overwhelming drawback to this system was that the decision could not be enforced, and, in early days, often led to a bloodier feud than might otherwise have occurred. In the reign of William III the practice of arbitration was legalized by statute.

The latest development in the evolution of law has already been shown to lie in the acceptance of the doctrine that what benefits the individual bene-

THE EVOLUTION OF STATE LAW. 93

fits the state; from which has resulted legislation devised to improve the conditions in which all classes of the community live.

Another important development, though of a more technical nature, is found in the Constitution of the United States, which provides for a federal or Supreme Court, whose judges, appointed by the President with the consent of the Senate, hold office "during good behaviour." The jurisdiction of this court is chiefly appellate. If a question involving the constitutionality of a law is submitted, it decides the matter; and if the act is considered unconstitutional, the federal court will not enforce it. Since the Act of Settlement in 1701, all the superior judges in Great Britain, appointed by the Crown, have held their offices "during good behaviour," and cannot be removed to suit political convenience. Since the reign of George III they have also continued to hold their appointments notwithstanding the demise of the Crown. They are disqualified from sitting in the House of Commons.

The following is a rough summary of the stages through which law has passed in reaching its present condition:

(1) Might the only remedy. Unrestrained fighting the only rule.

(2) More or less arbitrary intervention by some dominant power.

(3) The gradual recognition of precedent as worthy of consideration in connection with the tenure and conveyance of property; with a growing sense of honour and of similar sentiments resulting in rules regulating trial by combat.

(4) Voluntary submission of disputes to arbitration as an intermediate stage between the codification of the customs and rules of the third stage, and

(5) The enactment of laws by representatives of the people with permanent courts provided with legitimate means for the enforcement of these laws.

CHAPTER XI.

The Evolution of International Law.

THE evolution of International Law, so far as it has gone, has followed exactly the same course.

(1) At first, unbridled warfare was the only means conceived of for settling any dispute. Captives were slaughtered or sold into slavery; women were part of the spoils.

(2) Then, when this was found to interfere with neighbouring states or with the convenience of some dominant power, forcible intervention, accompanied, if necessary, by the same brutality, would put an end to the conflict. This interference would frequently lead to the spoliation of one or both parties to the original dispute. Sometimes, however, the intervening state would get the worst of it, and it was always possible that the two contending nations would unite temporarily to repel the uninvited mediator, to resume hostilities later, as between themselves, without fear of interruption.

When intervention took place peacefully it was on account of the overwhelming power of the self-appointed arbiter. Frequent examples of such intervention are found in the history of ancient Rome. Later, and after the third stage had been entered for a considerable time, the Pope would often mediate in order to prevent or stop warfare between the European States, and in this case it was not only his moral power that inspired awe, but an appreciation of the fact that at his bidding other nations might possibly come forward to make matters disagreeable for both factions. But his attempts at intervention did not always prove successful, as was shown by the failure of Boniface VIII to exercise his papal authority effectively in the disputes between France and England, and by England's defiance of his orders to abstain from all further attacks on Scotland. Boniface's capture by Philip of France was evidence that intervention by right of arbitrary might was a dangerous proceeding.

Mediating powers were in no case bound by any recognized code of law—not always by the facts—though they were influenced to a limited extent by public opinion and also took cognizance of precedent. In this way international customs began to be established.

(3) The third stage in the growth of law as between states, beginning, as said, long before the Popes had raised intervention to a fine art, was the gradual accumulation of precedent derived from

THE EVOLUTION OF INTERNATIONAL LAW. 97

treaties, truces, and other international compacts. These precedents were not collected in the form of a written code, but were considered more or less binding as custom. Humanitarian instincts, the influence of religion, and the fear of reprisals—a better understanding of self-interest and a sense of duty arising together—tended to introduce certain restraints in the waging and carrying on of wars. It came to be accepted, for instance, that a declaration or notice of war should be given to a previously friendly state.

(4) Arbitration was voluntarily resorted to, some king being asked to act as referee in disputed matters, though more often the Pope. Thus Henry II of England, on account of his power and character, was selected as arbitrator between Alphonso of Castile and Sancho of Navarre. Decisions given in this way were not based upon law, but upon the referee's understanding of equity and his interpretation and knowledge of custom.

Soon, however, students of state law, such as Francisco Suarez, began to collect these precedents, and in 1625 Hugo Grotius wrote his famous treatise on international law or custom, entitled *Jure Belli ac Pacis*. A treatise on international maritime law, entitled *Consulato del mare*, had been written at a much earlier date.

Since then, there has been less opportunity for

the action of what may be called caprice in the decisions given by arbitrators. They are bound by precedent as formulated by Grotius and more recent authorities, and are obliged to support their opinions by reference to treaties, such as those of Westphalia, Breda, Rastadt, Nystadt, Paris, Washington, and many others, in which the rights of nations have been to some extent defined. The "Alabama" claims, the Behring Sea fisheries quarrel, were settled in this way between the United States and Great Britain, while the Pope officiated as arbitrator between Germany and Spain, in 1885, in connection with the Caroline Islands.[1]

[1] Omitting earlier instances of arbitration, "the Congress of Vienna of 1815 left several questions to arbitration, such as the debt on the Rhine octrois, the succession to the duchy of Bouillon, the differences between the cantons of Ure and Tessin on the subject of custom-house and on a portion of the Dutch debt. In 1834-35 the King of Prussia arbitrated between France and England on the Portendic indemnity. In 1839 the Queen of England arbitrated between France and Mexico. In 1864 the Senate of Hamburg arbitrated between England and Peru. In 1869 the President of the United States arbitrated between England and Portugal. . . . In 1882 the claims of France and Italy against Chile for damages produced by her naval and military forces on their subjects were left to the arbitration of a mixed tribunal, consisting of persons nominated by the President of the French Republic (or by the King of Italy), the President of the Republic of Chile, and the Emperor of Brazil. In 1884 the claims of the United States against Hayti were left to the arbitration of the Hon. William Strong."—*International Law*, by L. Levi, chap. xxiii., § 404.

THE EVOLUTION OF INTERNATIONAL LAW. 99

But arbitration between nations is subject to the same drawback as was arbitration between individuals in England, before the reign of William III: the parties agreeing to the reference are not bound to conform to the decision rendered. If it suits them they can accept it; if it displeases them it can be rejected—as the United States rejected the award given against it in the matter of the British-American boundary dispute in 1831, and as some people in England wished to reject the award given against it in the matter of the "Alabama" claims.

This lack of power to enforce a decision, leaving the disputants to settle their affairs by trial by combat, would seem absurd and to the last degree barbarous in matters dealt with by state law. Imagine a decision of the courts in a dispute between the Governors of New York and Ohio, or between the Dukes of Westminster and Portland, being rejected by the parties concerned, and an immediate raising of troops to settle the quarrel after the fashion of the feudal barons! Yet that is exactly the condition of things which prevails today in international matters, and that is all that international law, so-called, can effect.

Is this "inevitable"? Is it "useless to look for any change so long as the passions of men are what they are"? But did no change take place in the Teutonic laws? Do laws depend upon the passions of men for their enactment? Are not intelligence and common sense as well developed to-day as they were five hundred years ago, when it was seen that for the benefit of every one concerned, passions should be restrained by law and if necessary by dispassionate force, subject to law? Is the policy of inaction still omnipotent? Have not people come to realize that nothing in nature can remain stationary, but must move onward in the course of evolution?

A comparison of the stages passed in the development of international and state law respectively, up to the present time, is most significant:

STATE OR MUNICIPAL LAW.	INTERNATIONAL LAW.
(1) Might the only remedy. Unrestrained fighting the only rule.	(1) Might the only remedy. Unrestrained fighting the only rule.
(2) More or less arbitrary intervention by some dominant power.	(2) More or less arbitrary intervention by some dominant power.
(3) The gradual recognition of precedent as worthy of consideration in connection with the tenure and conveyance	(3) The gradual recognition of precedent as worthy of consideration in connection with the tenure and conveyance

of property, with a growing sense of honour and of similar sentiments, resulting in rules regulating trial by combat, such as that notice of intention to fight should be given.

(4) Voluntary submission of disputes to arbitration, without power to enforce decisions, as an intermediate stage between the codification of the customs and rules of the third stage, *and*

(5) The enactment of laws by representatives of the people with permanent courts provided with legitimate means for the enforcement of these laws.

of property (territory, etc.), with a growing sense of honour and of similar sentiments, resulting in rules regulating trial by warfare, such as that notice of intention to fight should be given.

(4) Voluntary submission of disputes to arbitration, without power to enforce decisions, as an intermediate stage between the codification of the customs and rules of the third stage, *and*

What must be the next step in the evolution of International Law? Do not reason and experience alike answer the question? Does not every ethical concept demand that this step should be taken, and does not self-interest in its turn proclaim its needs?—The enactment of laws by representatives of the nations with permanent courts provided with legitimate means for the enforcement of these laws.

Part Fourth.
A PRACTICAL MEASURE.

CHAPTER XII.

Its General Character.

THAT all the nations claiming to be civilized would unite in enacting laws through their representatives, and in establishing a permanent court provided with legitimate means for the enforcement of such laws, is almost unthinkable; but that *some* will do this is rather more than probable. The bare suggestion, when at first formally submitted, will provoke a storm of objection, even in those countries where it is destined to meet with the most support and with comparatively quick adoption.

But before attempting to deal with these objections, obvious as they are from a superficial point of view, it will be well to elaborate somewhat the essential idea under consideration, and then to follow up the inquiry made in a previous chapter—determining the extent to which the principle of interdependence has already been recognized by the great Powers—by pointing out the important beginnings that have even now been made by the

Powers in applying the principle in the practical way suggested. It will in any case become evident that the measure proposed—that of establishing international laws in fact as well as in name—would not be a sudden or radical departure, and would only necessitate, in the first place, the formal recognition of certain practices, which have been inaugurated already, as duties unconditionally binding upon civilized nations.

The off-hand criticism, which is sure to be passed, that the whole idea is Utopian, need not be seriously considered. Prejudice and ignorance once condemned the idea of representative government as Utopian; every next step in the evolution of anything, until it is taken, is labelled Utopian. Labels do not affect laws of growth; ignorance and consequent scepticism cannot alter the fact that an ugly green caterpillar develops into a butterfly; and if it be suggested that the growth of human law is peculiar, inasmuch as it is subject to the desires of man, it may fairly be answered that the desires of man are subject to the laws of universal nature. It might be supposed that the apparently vacillating desires of man would make such a thing as marriage incapable of being reduced to any rule by which the number of marriages taking place in a year could be calculated beforehand; and yet national statistics prove that their occurrence can be calculated beforehand, and that they take place according to constant natural laws. The growth of human law is not peculiar. Men in the mass do not depart from their own record; and it is because civilized man is ready for the change in question—has been working up to it for centuries—that the change is sure to come.

Jeremy Bentham cannot be accused of taking an optimistic or idealistic view of his fellow-men, and his well-known definition of the impracticable is almost sufficient in itself as an answer to the "Utopian" objection. "There is one case in which, in a certain sense, a plan may be said to be too good to be practicable, and that case a very comprehensive one. It is where, without adequate inducement in the shape of personal interest, the plan requires for its accomplishment that some individual or class of individuals shall have made a sacrifice of his or their personal interest to the interest of the whole." To such a plan, "the term 'Utopian' may without impropriety be applied."[1]

Virtually no sacrifice of "personal interest" to the interest of the whole will be required in this case, while more than "adequate inducement in the shape of personal interest" can be offered.

[1] *The Book of Fallacies*, by Jeremy Bentham. "Fallacies of Confusion," chap. ix., § 4.

CHAPTER XIII.

Its First Clause.

THE first clause of the measure under consideration is: *That nations should unite in enacting laws through their representatives,* just as individuals have for long united in doing the same thing.

This has already been accomplished to a certain extent. What has been done only needs to be carried further. International Conventions or Congresses have frequently been held, and at these, not only rules governing international relationships have been agreed to, but principles of law, in the highest and best sense, have been enunciated.

Rules for the navigation of rivers separating or traversing several States were laid down by the Congress of Vienna in 1815. A "Declaration of Maritime Law" was agreed to at the Congress of Paris of 1856, and the rights and duties of neutrals then defined were further elaborated in the Treaty of Washington in 1870. What may be called rules for the conduct of war were framed at the

Geneva Convention of 1864, in a declaration signed at St. Petersburg in 1868, and, tentatively, in the proposed Declaration of Brussels. A "Universal Postal Union" was established by treaty in 1874 (enlarged and modified in subsequent years). International rules were agreed to, at a Convention held at Paris in 1874, for the protection of submarine telegraph cables. Rules concerning industrial property, including patents, trademarks, etc., were established by nearly all the Powers at a Convention held at Paris in 1883. Rules regulating navigation were adopted at the International Marine Conference held at Washington in 1889.[1]

In the protocol signed at the Conference of London of 1871, the representatives of Russia, Austria, France, Germany, Great Britain, Italy, and Turkey, stated that they recognized it to be a principle of international law that no power can avoid the fulfilment of treaties, or alter their stipulations, unless with the consent of the contracting parties voluntarily given. The Clayton-Bulwer Treaty of 1850, between the United States and Great Britain, professed to "establish a general principle" of law.

Even ethical principles have received recognition, as well as principles of law. One noticeable instance of this is to be found in the "Declaration

[1] See Note F., on "The International Marine Conference." This Conference was called by the United States.

of the Powers on the Abolition of the Slave Trade" (*Traite des Nègres*), at the Congress of Vienna, in 1815, according to the terms of which,—

"The Plenipotentiaries of the Powers who signed the Treaty of Paris of May 30, 1814, united in Conference, having taken into consideration that the commerce known as the African Slave-Trade *has been held by just and enlightened men of all times as repugnant to the principles of humanity and universal morals;*

" . . . That the Plenipotentiaries assembled at the Congress could not better honour their missions, fulfil their duties, and manifest the principles which guide their august Sovereigns, than . . . in proclaiming in the name of their Sovereigns the wish to put an end to an evil which has for so long desolated Africa, degraded Europe, and afflicted humanity;—

"The said Plenipotentiaries are agreed to deliberate upon the means for accomplishing an object so salutary by a solemn declaration of the principles which guided them in this labour.

"Consequently, . . . they declare in the face of Europe that, regarding the universal abolition of the Slave-Trade as a measure especially worthy of their attention, in conformity with the spirit of the age and the generous principles of their august Sovereigns, they are animated by the sincere desire of concurring in the execution of the shortest and most efficacious measure by every means in their power, and to act in the use of such means with all the zeal and all the perseverance which they owe to so great and beautiful a cause. . . . "[1]

This remarkable declaration (rather surprising in its morality) was signed by all the participants in the Congress, representing Austria, Spain, France, Great Britain, Portugal and Brazil, Prussia, Russia, and Sweden and Norway.

There is one point of vital importance to be borne in mind in connection with these international rules or laws: that unanimity of consent is not necessary in order to insure unanimous recognition of the rule. Thus, although neither the United States, Spain, nor Mexico agreed to the Declaration of Paris abolishing privateering, they are nevertheless almost as much bound by the terms of that declaration as if they had signed it. As late as 1895, Portugal and Brazil, Mexico and other South American Republics had not agreed to the provisions of the Geneva Convention; but a violation of its rules by any one of those states would undoubtedly meet with protest, probably supported by force, on the part of the other Powers. Experience has proved that any declaration of international law by two or more states, such as that

[1] See *International Law*, by Levi, p. 301.

contained in the Treaty of Washington between the United States and Great Britain—always supposing that it embodies sound principles and seems likely to prove generally beneficial—will soon be adopted, if only by silent consent, by all the civilized nations. More often the adoption will be formal.

There has always been a considerable lapse of time between the original signing of such treaties embodying laws, and their ratification by states other than the original signatories. It was not until 1862 that practically all the great Powers had given effect to the Declaration concerning the Slave-Trade, of 1815; and although the Convention of Geneva was held in 1864, its provisions were not formally acceded to by the United States until 1882.

It follows, therefore, that if only two or three nations combined at the present time to formulate a Code of International Law, if such a code were just and reasonable in its provisions, it would become practically binding upon all the civilized Powers.[1]

[1] In formulating such a Code, the "high contracting parties" could hardly do better than take some concise state code, such as the *Code Napoléon*, with its five parts—viz., the *Code Civil*, the *Code de Procédure Civile*, the *Code de Commerce*, the *Code d'Instruction Criminelle*, and the *Code Pénal*—and interpret in terms applying to nations the laws framed for the benefit of individuals, so far as this might be deemed necessary or useful.

ITS FIRST CLAUSE.

One of the first cares of the international legislators would of necessity be the recognition and protection of the absolute autonomy of participating states, for the object of law is not only to define and safeguard rights, but to insure *liberties*. If state law were to attempt any interference with the acts of a man which do not directly affect other individuals or the community as a whole, it would outrage every canon of personal freedom. In the same way, international law would be strictly confined to international relationships.

The limits of justifiable interference in the acts of individuals have been fairly well determined. Such acts must demonstrably affect the community before the law can take cognizance of them. Suicide, for example, is held to affect the community injuriously, in so far as it unnecessarily and evilly deprives the state of a citizen. Suicide is a murderous act committed by an individual upon himself, and the law warrants intervention accordingly. If the internal conduct of a state were such that its very existence as a state were threatened, as by a civil war carried on for so long or so barbarously that the extermination of both parties were to appear probable, international law, founded upon the principles outlined, would warrant interference, and, if necessary, the subjection of the country to temporary restraint. But only in such extreme circumstances would international law, so founded, be applicable to domestic affairs; a conclusion which prevailing international custom supports.

It may be suggested as significant, however, that state law is less constrained in its dealings with a man's treatment of his own household than it is in connection with what are sometimes described as his "self-regarding" acts, or acts which are alleged to affect himself only—if such be conceivable. Gross ill-treatment by parents of their offspring, or of servants by their employers (formerly of slaves by their owners), is punishable, and would be prevented even though there might seem to be no immediate danger that the ill-treatment would result in death. For state law distinguishes between an individual and those whom he controls—those whom he would perhaps claim to own; and international law would distinguish between a civil war on the one hand, and war between a country and its colonies, or a rebellion by a conquered people against its rulers, on the other. International custom approves this discrimination also.

Once these distinguishing features were defined, and the legal and philosophical principles upon which such differences really depend were formulated, intervention, instead of being the arbitrary act of some neighbouring state, would be the legitimate enforcement of a law by the lawmaking Powers, whenever the conditions no longer warranted an attitude of strict neutrality.

Another important matter requiring consideration in an International Code would be the ownership of unoccupied territory, the right to acquire it, the terms upon which it might be acquired, and so forth, as well as the conditions necessary to validate the leasing or purchase of territory or other property from uncivilized peoples, in regard to which the most hopeless confusion prevails at the present time, leading to constant friction and dangerous *contretemps* between the nations. Trading rights should also be defined. It would perhaps be decided to make trade with the remaining nondescript territories, such as portions of China and Africa which have not as yet been stolen by the Powers, free to all comers.

But this is neither the time nor the place for submitting a detailed international application of the legal and philosophical principles in question. The application is easy once the principles are grasped. Nor would it be necessary for the representatives of the Powers participating in a legislative Convention to admit the soundness of these principles. No matter upon what they might base their action, it is manifestly of the first importance that a legal code should be formulated and accepted, regulating the relations of states in as many respects as possible, instead of confining itself to the few matters which international "law" already covers, such as maritime procedure, the conduct of war, and so forth. "The law of nature is, Do the thing, and you shall have the power; but they who do not the thing have not the power." The formulation of right laws is in itself a revelation of right principle.

Failing right principle, a mere codification of custom, after the style of the laws of Ælfred, would be better than nothing to begin with, so long as it were formally agreed to by some of the great Powers, and so long as the establishment of permanent courts provided with legitimate means for the enforcement of such laws were made part of the measure. Even the proper regulation of trial by combat would be a step in the right direction, strange as the admission sounds in the nineteenth century. To take steps to confine warfare on land to the contending armies, sparing as much as possible the non-combatants, the women, and the children, by leaving the crops, the water supply, and private dwelling-houses intact, would at least bring international conflicts nearer the standard of modern duellists, who would consider it monstrous to set fire to each other's houses.

Still, it is scarcely conceivable that the civilized

nations would be content to let the matter rest there, once they were to give it their serious attention, and once the pressing need for international legislation were brought home to the great mass of the people, with whom the responsibility for the solution of the question will ultimately rest, and who will demand the formulation of a proper Code, for their own peace and security. Precedent, taken by itself, will not be considered sufficient or satisfactory; and it is doubtful whether a fitting basis for a Code could be found apart from the long experience already gained in state law. By reasoning from the individual to the nation, remembering that a nation is an individual for all legal intents and purposes, the representatives of the Powers in Convention assembled could draw up a Code, which, in the course of time, after ratification by the Governments respectively represented, would inevitably become the world's law.

Whatever results might be arrived at in the first place, could be in no sense final, and further assemblies might be held at stated intervals in order to revise the original ordinances. International law would continue to develop, just as state law undergoes modification in proportion to the growing perceptions of individuals. We may be sure that as the whole trend of evolution has been working up to this minor climax in the life of humanity, once a deliberate beginning is made, progress will be steady and sure.

The first step is a Conference; then to get two or three of the nations represented to agree upon a Code; and the rest would virtually follow of its own accord.

CHAPTER XIV.

Its Second Clause.

THE second clause of the measure proposed is that when enacting laws through their representatives, *the nations should also establish a permanent court to adjudicate upon all international questions which could not be settled amicably*, as between those nations giving formal adherence to the Code.

This, again, has already been accomplished to a certain extent; what has been done only needs to be carried further.

It may be argued that the appointment of arbitrators to settle a specific question is in no way a precedent for the establishment and maintenance of a permanent court. It may further be held that Article VIII of the Treaty of Paris of 1856, for instance, did not constitute the signatory Powers a permanent tribunal for the settlement of any differences between Turkey and the other Powers, though that is what the wording of the article actually implies—for "if there should arise between the Sublime Porte and one or more of the signing

Powers, any misunderstanding which might endanger the maintenance of their relations, the Sublime Porte and each of such Powers, before having recourse to the use of force, shall afford the other contracting parties the opportunity of preventing such an extremity by means of their mediation."

Ample and explicit precedent for the establishment of such a court is to be found, nevertheless, as in the protocol appended to the Treaty of Commerce and Navigation between Great Britain and Italy, signed at Rome in 1883, according to the terms of which:

"Any controversies which may arise respecting the interpretation or the execution of the present Treaty, or the consequences of any violation thereof, shall be submitted, when the means of settling them directly by amicable agreement are exhausted, to the decision of commissions of arbitration, and the result of such arbitration shall be binding upon both Governments.

"The members of such commissions shall be selected by the two Governments by common consent, failing which, each of the parties shall nominate an arbitrator, or an equal number of arbitrators, and the arbitrators thus appointed shall select an umpire."

This provision for the settlement of all differences whatsoever arising from the interpretation of a treaty, by a tribunal duly provided for, actually constitutes a permanent court, to become kinetic, as it were, with comparatively little delay.

According to Levi, "The Convention of Paris of 1873 (Art. XVIII), for a Universal Postal Union, has a provision to the effect that in case of disagreement between two or more members of the union as to the interpretation of the Convention, the question in dispute is to be decided by arbitration."

"The pact of union between Costa Rica, Guatemala, Honduras, and Salvador [self-governing states], dated February 17th, 1872, Article III, provides: The maintenance of peace between the Central American Republics is a strict duty of their respective Governments, and any differences which may arise between them, whatever be the cause, will be settled amicably by means of the mediation of the Governments which are not parties to the difference. In cases where the difference remains unsettled, the same shall be left to the arbitration either of the Central American authority which shall be afterwards established, or to the judgment of a tribunal of arbitration, composed of representatives of the neutral Central American Governments. The Government or Governments which shall infringe this principle will be guilty of treason against the Central American nations." [1]

[1] *International Law*, by Leone Levi, chap. xxiii., § 417.

These agreements afford further precedents for what is proposed, though common sense should make precedent almost superfluous. The same circumstances that make a permanent Court desirable in matters of state procedure, hold good in the field of international complications. The appointment of arbitrators for special purposes is not only a cumbersome and lengthy proceeding, involving dangerous delay and giving scope for an increase of friction between the parties at issue, but is contrary to the best principles of jurisprudence, according to which immediate relief should be obtainable for just cause, at any time, by all persons.

It has also been found that men whose sole business it is to interpret the law, who hold office for life or "during good behaviour," and whose positions and future employment in no way depend upon the nature of the decisions they give, are more likely to be impartial and impersonal in their justice than those who, appointed for a brief period or subject to dismissal without due cause, are almost sure to be affected by a consciousness of the results to themselves if they should give a decision adverse to the interests of those who appointed them.

An International Supreme Court would therefore have to be established. It might consist of a fixed number of judges to be named by the representatives of the Powers when assembled for legislative purposes, or by the Heads of States, without regard for the nationality of the appointees; or it might consist of a varying number, one or more judges being appointed by the Governments of each participating country. These judges would naturally be men of unimpeachable probity, and in the event of it being thought better that they should not be lawyers, a permanent Advisory Council could be established, consisting of lawyers whose only duty it would be to advise the Court on points of law.

The Court would have to be held in some neutral city, such as Geneva or Cairo; perhaps at St. Helena.

All matters laid before the Court for decision would have to be submitted by the Heads of States. It could deal with them only, for it would be concerned with nations, not with individuals, and the Government of each country would be responsible for the maintenance of order, under the provisions of its own law, within its own territories.

CHAPTER XV.

Its Third Clause.

THE last clause of the measure may seem to be a departure from custom: that *this permanent Court should be provided with means to enforce its decisions.* Precedent, however, again shows that the departure would not be radical, but would be a consecutive move along a line of procedure already established.

For the proposition simply comes to this: that the law-making Powers shall mutually agree to give reality to their own laws by guaranteeing their enforcement. They would first formulate their Code of law, then agree by regular Treaty to conform to it, and then undertake to enforce the provisions of the Treaty thus entered into.

Such a compact has frequently been made in the past. It has become a recognized mode of procedure, and receives due attention at the hands of all writers on International Law. Thus Hall explains (Part II, chap. x., § 113) that "Treaties of guarantee are agreements through which powers engage, either by an independent treaty to maintain a given state of things, or by a treaty or provisions accessory to a treaty, to secure the stipulations of the latter from infraction by the use of such means as may be specified or required against a country acting adversely to such stipulations." He cites as an instance of guarantee the Treaty of April 15th, 1856, by which England, Austria, and France guaranteed "jointly and severally the independence and the integrity of the Ottoman Empire, recorded in the treaty concluded at Paris on the 30th March"; and also the treaties of 1831 and 1839, "by which Belgium was constituted an independent and neutral state in the common interests of the contracting powers, and while placed under an obligation to maintain neutrality, received a guarantee that it should be enabled to do so." So long ago as 1648 a Treaty of this kind was entered into by France and Sweden, to prevent the Peace of Westphalia from being violated by the Germans or by the Austrians.[1]

The important difference between these Treaties of Guarantee and what is now proposed is that, instead of it being left to the contracting parties to enforce the laws they have agreed to, at their own convenience, or not at all, it shall be the duty of the International Court to enforce its own deci-

[1] Bowen, § 120.

sions; further, the law-making Powers shall put means at the disposal of the Court to enable this to be done.

How unsatisfactory an ordinary Treaty of Guarantee is, may be judged from a plea put forward by Lord Derby in 1867, that a collective guarantee means that in the event of a treaty being violated, "all the powers who have signed the treaty may be called upon for their collective action. No one of those powers is liable to be called upon to act singly or separately. . . . We are bound in honour —you cannot place a legal construction upon it— to see in concert with others that these arrangements are maintained. But if the other powers join with us, it is certain that there will be no violation. . . . *If they, situated exactly as we are, decline to join, we are not bound single-handed to make up the deficiency.*" [1]

Imagine the laws of the United States, for example, depending for their enforcement upon the possible preferences and inclinations of its private citizens in some particular case! They would cease to be laws; they would become rules, but with less authority than rules of baseball, which an umpire is at least sometimes able to enforce by sheer might of avoirdupois.

Imagine, again, that the Courts were obliged to

[1] Quoted by Hall, Part II., chap. x., § 113.

refer in each instance to the law-making power, whether a representative assembly or an autocratic ruler, in order to have their decisions made effective: it would open each case afresh, leading to infinite delay and to constant perversions of justice, besides reducing the Courts to the position of intermediaries, instead of constituting them direct agents, as is necessary if their authority is to be respected.

Upon the right settlement of this question entirely depends the practical value of international legislation. The weak spot in the armour of arbitration has always been that decisions so obtained cannot be made final. It is open to the contending parties to accept or reject these decisions as they may happen to prefer; and if war should follow arbitration, the delay resulting therefrom and the discussions arising from the negotiations could but add fuel to the fire, bitterness to the contest.[1]

[1] This was the fatal flaw in the proposed Treaty of Arbitration of 1897 between the United States and Great Britain. In its original condition it was a sort of friendly flourish, but beyond that it was not worth the paper it was written on. After maceration at the hands of the Senate Committee on Foreign Relations, the good sense of both nations awoke to the Treaty's deficiencies; and, failing a proper solution of the matter, the Senate refused to ratify it, for although forty-three Senators voted in favor of ratification and only twenty-six voted against it, the measure failed to obtain endorsement, as an affirmative vote of two-thirds of the Senators voting was necessary to ratification.

It is quite evident that law which exists on paper only, which has no "strong arm" to back it, is almost worse than useless, seeing that it is likely to inspire contempt—if it inspires notice of any sort —and certainly cannot inspire respect. Without the "strong arm" it is an empty form; with the "strong arm" it is the mainstay of order, of justice, of peace and prosperity.

How the Court should be provided with means to enforce its decisions is another matter, though the solution of the problem is easily found: it should be done as nearly as possible in the same way that national courts are provided with similar means. There is an Executive as well as a Judicial and a Legislative side to the law.

It would be unprofitable to enter now into details concerning the differences between the functions of the sheriff and the constabulary in the administration of the English and American law, or to attempt to outline the application of the same practice on an international scale. Nor would it be of present service to show the evolution of one of the executive branches of the law up to its modern high standard of excellence. "Yet the stages of growth are sufficiently well marked—from the responsibility of the tithing to the responsibility of its head, from the functions of the head borough or tithing-man to the functions of the constable, from the election of

ITS THIRD CLAUSE. 129

a constable to the election of a plurality of constables, deputy constables, and watchmen, under parochial or other local authority, to a plurality of constables under the central authority of a Secretary of State"[1]—as in the London Metropolitan Police system.

Nor would it be of any avail to consider whether this system is or is not preferable to that prevailing in countries more directly influenced by Roman Law, in which the *gendarmerie* have judicial as well as executive functions. Some modification of one or the other system will probably be applied *ultimately* to the international situation. These future developments will take care of themselves, however.

The only point requiring immediate attention is the extent to which the principle could be practically and wisely applied at the present time.

Let it be supposed that a certain number of nations were to take part in a Conference for the purpose of considering the present condition of International Law. The representatives attending the Conference would report to their respective Governments the result of their deliberations, and some of them possibly would submit the draft of an International Code, covering such points as it had been deemed necessary or wise to cover. After

[1] *History of Crime in England*, vol. ii., p. 460, by L. O. Pike.

this Code had been amended by the participating Governments, it would be referred back to the Conference, adjourned for that purpose; a revised Code would be drafted, would be again submitted to the Governments for ratification, and, no matter how long it might take, would finally be adopted.

The greater the number of participating Powers, the longer it would take to obtain its ratification; so, from one point of view, it would be better in the first place to have two or three countries co-operating than to have many. Once such a Code were adopted, other civilized states would very soon accept its provisions, if only for their own protection and benefit.

According to the terms of the Code, the appointment of Judges or permanent arbitrators would then be made, in either of the ways already referred to under that head. Upon the terms of the Code would also depend the method by which the Court, thus constituted, could give effect to its decisions. Probably the same system would be adopted as that which prevailed in state law before the present elaborate system had been perfected; that is to say, the Court would give its decision, and on the complaint of one of the parties that the terms of the decision had not been complied with, the Court would take steps to investigate the matter, and, if the complaint were justified by the facts, would then inform the Heads of the Governments of the "high contracting parties" to the Code that, according to the terms of that Code, it had become their duty to enforce the Court's decision, and that, if necessary, they should immediately use their land and naval forces for that purpose.

Thus, if the United Kingdom of Great Britain and Ireland and the Colonies, Sweden and Norway, Holland, some other Continental Powers, the United States of America, and Japan and Mexico, were the "high contracting parties" in question, and in a dispute between Mexico and Japan the former country refused to obey the order of the Court thereupon, the Court would notify the Queen of Great Britain and Ireland, the President of the United States, and the heads of the other states concerned (representing for the nonce the "county sheriffs" of some countries), that it had become their duty to give effect to the decision of the Court. It would then rest with them to decide by which of the means already recognized by international law this could be done in the most effective and most humane manner.

In the unlikely event that Mexico, in this case, would remain obdurate, it would by no means follow that war would have to be declared against her: war would only result if Mexico herself were foolish enough to declare for it, and in that event the penalty for resisting the law by force would be severe—a penalty determined by the Court according to the provisions of the Code.

Violence could only result from resistance—a fact of very great consequence. Other methods have for long been employed, and would doubtless be employed again in an emergency like the one under consideration. An embargo suspending commerce with the offending nation, or a pacific blockade of the nation's ports, such as that maintained in 1827 on the coasts of Greece and very frequently since then in other cases; these and other more peaceful methods could be resorted to, and would probably prove sufficient to compel obedience to the behests of the law. But once the "strong arm" were known to be ready, it would rarely have to be used, and self-respecting nations would in any case be law-abiding.

Ultimately—no matter how far off that day may be—when the large majority of the civilized nations will have united in acceding to the then existing Code of International Law, though discord and strife will by no means have left the earth, there will be one law for the weak and the strong alike among nations—at least to the same extent that it may now be said that the same law protects both the rich and the poor in properly governed communities.

By then the employment of force will doubtless have been reduced to a minimum, though it will still have to be used occasionally; for just as the civilized majority in any state is obliged to protect itself against the uncivilized minority, so the majority of the nations will perhaps find it necessary to defend themselves occasionally against the encroachments of marauding barbarians (from near or far). Small standing armies and navies will probably have to be maintained by each of the states, in proportion to their total population, in order to preserve order within their own territories as well as to act as the executive arm of the International Court. But these forces will not stand in constant readiness to act against each other as they do at present. They will still be national; they will remain under the control of their own Governments; but it will be their duty to co-operate for the preservation of order, should the occasion arise, as the police of different cities and even of different nations already co-operate in the prevention and punishment of crime.

For this reason their number would not need to be large; for if only one in every thousand of the population of Europe and America were to belong to these standing forces, they could collectively control the hordes of China if called upon to do so as International Police.

However remote such a relatively ideal condition of things may seem to be, it would involve no greater development than that which has taken place in England during the past four hundred years; and the world moves far more rapidly to-day than it did formerly. There is now a much closer union between London and San Francisco than there was between London and Edinburgh four hundred years ago. Evolution is constant, but its pace varies; and once its stages have been traversed, they can be repeated on a larger scale in an astonishingly brief period.

Darwin produced species of pigeons in a few years that centuries could not have produced without the assistance of his guiding mind; and when men come to realize the goal toward which international affairs are wending, when they appreciate the laws that govern the progress of nations, they will, like Darwin, deliberately repeat in a very short time, on an international scale, what it has taken centuries to produce on a smaller scale in ignorance of the process taking place.

The future, however, as said already, will largely take care of itself. What will not take care of itself, what imperiously calls for attention, is the present moment and the duty of that moment. If from moment to moment the right step be taken, all will go well. The past and the future can be usefully considered in so far as they throw light upon this next step, and, in the domain of international activity, both past and future point to the urgent need of holding a Convention of representatives of the nations to consider the condition of what now passes current as International Law.[1]

[1] See Note G., on "Sully and Kant."

CHAPTER XVI.

Some Possible Objections.

It will possibly be objected that the enactment of international laws by nations would interfere with the freedom of action of nations, considered in their separate character. Exactly the same objection has been made, by some writers, to the enactment of state laws: they would rather leave men free to do whatever they like. This is an old question; it has been thrashed out till there is nothing left of it but a damaged note of interrogation.

If people will ask themselves how they would have liked to live in a country devoid of law and of order, where evil was unrestrained, where the strong ruled the weak and the strongest ruled the strong, they may reach a practical solution of the problem, apart from philosophical argument. Let it not be forgotten, however, that any such objection as that suggested at once raises the further question, What is Freedom? License is not liberty; disorder does not favour growth: animals with social instincts have learned that much. In the words of Hegel:

SOME POSSIBLE OBJECTIONS. 137

"Limitation is certainly produced by Society and the State, but it is a limitation of the mere brute emotions and rude instincts; as also, in a more advanced stage of culture, of the premeditated self-will of caprice and passion. This kind of constraint is part of the instrumentality by which only the Consciousness of Freedom and the desire for its attainment, in its true—that is Rational and Ideal—form, can be obtained. To the Ideal of Freedom, Law and Morality are indispensably requisite. . . ."[1]

No man is free who violates natural (universal) law, because its violation means that he is seized by it, and becomes the slave of the penalties involved in his own deed.

In conformity with natural law man enacts hu-

[1] *Philosophy of History*, Introduction, III., 3, translated by J. Sibree. In Herbert Spencer's article on "Evolutionary Ethics," in *Appleton's Popular Science Monthly* for February, 1898 (to which reference is made in Note C., on "The Morality of the Evolutionary Process"), he says, speaking of his own teaching: "I am not aware that any one has more emphatically asserted that society in its corporate capacity must exercise a rigorous control over its individual members, to the extent needful for preventing trepasses one upon another. No one has more frequently or strongly denounced governments for the laxity with which they fulfil this duty. So far from being, as some have alleged, an advocacy of the claims of the strong against the weak, it is much more an insistence that the weak shall be guarded against the strong, so that they may suffer no greater evils than their relative weakness itself involves."

man laws, and to these he should likewise conform, for it is their object to protect the rights and preserve the liberties of himself and his fellows; and if existing laws do not succeed in this, then it is for him to alter them, so that they may become more truly representative of freedom: for without law, freedom is impossible.

In a community of perfect men—if such be conceivable—human law would doubtless be unnecessary, for each member of the community would be wise as well as good, and, knowing the nature of the universe, would express in all his acts the ideal of law. But until humanity becomes perfect we shall have to put up with make-shifts in the place of perfect men, and must, at the least, place some restraint upon positive wrong-doing. This is the conclusion arrived at even by certain races otherwise savage; and the more civilized a state becomes, the more fully does it recognize that restraint of evil-doing is necessary, that rights have to be protected, liberties preserved.

That which applies to individuals applies to nations. The small restraints imposed by the nations upon themselves by the enactment of international laws would ensure freedom, and could never detract from it.

If, however, it should be argued with brutal frankness (also with some disregard for facts),

"We are a great Power; we are strong enough to get our own way in any circumstances, and need not care about justice so long as we can do what we choose"—it may be suggested that "great Powers" are liable to be met and even to be overcome by combinations of other Powers, and that it would be well to insure against that possibility by using some of a country's strength, while it has it, in establishing justice on a firm basis, and by enacting laws which will prevent the unwarrantable subjection of the weak by the strong. Life insurance is thought well of by most business people.

Another objection, sure to be raised, is that law, a central tribunal and so forth, would tend to weaken if not to destroy patriotism. But again definition is important. For what is patriotism? Is it a love of the best in one's country—a love of one's country because, whether rightly or wrongly, one believes it to be the best? Or is it a love of one's country simply because it is one's own? And if the latter is the case, as it generally is, should our love compel us to defy morality and justice on our country's behalf, or should we desire to see it conform to right principle and to the exigencies of universal law, if only for its own safety and well-being?

A contributor to the literature on this subject, a

vehement defender of patriotism, has sought to strengthen his position by asking why, if it may be said morally, "My mother, right or wrong!", "My country, right or wrong!" is not an equally moral exclamation.

Taking this as an unequivocal declaration of what passes for patriotic sentiment, it would seem all the more evident that while we support the mother, "right or wrong," we should desire her to go right and to keep right; and that we should use our utmost influence with that in view for the very reason that we love her best of all. The more ardent the patriot, the more anxious he should be to see his country one of the first to adapt itself to changed conditions and to the needs of the hour. If he can go no further than to admit that honesty is the best policy in the long run, he should endeavour to induce his country to act accordingly. If, furthermore, he follows the evolution of state law, and comes to the conclusion that the next step for the more highly civilized nations to take is cooperation in the enactment of international laws, his patriotism alone should impel him to try to make his own country (as the *most* civilized from his point of view) the first to support the movement.

Would he thereby become less patriotic? One might as reasonably ask whether the enactment of laws by individuals, and their conformity thereto, is apt to make them dangerously unselfish! The objection is in fact absurd. To join with others in some legislative undertaking gives rise at the most to a feeling of clannishness among the participants, but one finds that the members of the clan are in no great haste to give way to each other; they desire to see themselves and their immediate coterie first and foremost in the association.

It would be the same with nations taking part in this wider movement, and with the individuals composing those nations; though one may hope that in the course of time the patriotic sentiments of individuals would find vent in striving to make their country great in its mental and moral development, healthy in mind and body, rather than a first class rough-and-tumble fighter among the nations, with morals nowhere and mind cultivated for offensive and defensive purposes only.

Law among nations would immensely increase patriotism, in the best sense of the word. It could never diminish it.

Quite a different kind of objection may be put forward by those who would have peace at any price, and who look upon the exercise of force by one nation upon another as wholly evil.

The question is whether they would abolish

State law altogether, or whether they would, on the other hand, uphold State law and countenance the use of force in its support. It is well to be consistent in such matters. It is also well to remember that to use force for one's own personal protection is one thing, and that to use it for the protection of the weak and the oppressed is quite another. To use force for the last-named purpose is, in principle, the same thing as to use it in order to uphold law and order.

One can cordially sympathize with those who set an enormous value on peace and who strive by every means in their power to promote it. The barbarous brutality of war can never be sufficiently emphasized. In the remote future, when it has become a subject for historical research, along with gladiatorial combats and human sacrifices, its iniquities should still be held up as a warning to the human race. To say that it never produces anything but evil, however, would give the lie to the lessons of nature, for good does come out of evil, though evil is always left behind in the process. But to admit a percentage of good in a mass of evil is not to endorse the evil, and the most violent partisans of war can scarcely deny the overwhelming blessings of peace.

How best to promote it is the question then, and the answer is to be found in the solution of the

SOME POSSIBLE OBJECTIONS. 143

same problem by and as between individuals. It is not sufficient to preach and to teach. Practical effect must be given to the ethical ideal; and in the present state of civilization, no matter what the future may bring forth, the best and most practical public expression of the ethical ideal is to be found in legislation, by nations as by individuals.

Some people, judging hastily, may say that the proposal in general is good enough as a theory, but——. The rest will not be defined in words, for the average Anglo-Saxon mind has a vast distrust of theories, so vast and so deep-seated that the mere suspicion of one produces a clammy silence, not to be overcome. The people of Great Britain and of the United States alike pride themselves on being a commercial race, practical and not theoretical. Progress cannot be made to order, it is said; it must result from the slow pushing of events.

All of which is excellent, so far as it goes. Such an attitude of mind is at least a safeguard against experimental visionaries. But the foundation in reason for such an attitude is that experience should be the guide of conduct, not theory; or that theory should in any case be most strictly checked by the facts of experience; and as the measure now proposed does not depend upon either theory or experience alone, but upon either apart from the other, or upon both jointly, it should come up to the standard of the most practical person's requirements, particularly as events seem to have conspired to precipitate its accomplishment.

Simplicity of appeal counts for much with most people, especially with traders, and to the trader it may be said with sufficient directness: You as a trader know that it is necessary in your business to live in the midst of law and order. You could not get along without law in your own country; it has become necessary to your existence. There is no international law, and there ought to be, for you are concerned in the commerce of all nations; and if you have managed to get along in the past without it, somehow, your experience at home proves how much better you would get along with it. It follows that you should use the whole of your influence, both at home and abroad, to have a Conference called to discuss the matter; and that you should see to it that the right steps are taken by the national representatives to improve the present state of affairs.

CHAPTER XVII.

CONCLUSION.

IF it can be shown in answer to the objection already referred to—the off-hand condemnation of the measure in question as Utopian and impossible of fulfilment—that virtually no sacrifice of "personal interest" to the interest of the whole will be required in order to give it effect, while more than "adequate inducement in the shape of personal interest" can be offered, even Bentham's utilitarianism would pronounce the proposition as not only practicable, but as practically irresistible.

Nations are now governed by the mass of their population. That is self-evident. The great ear of the peoples is sometimes slow in hearing; their voice pauses long before it proclaims their will; but nothing can withstand the inevitable hour of their awakening, and when they move the whole world moves with them. It is the same in small matters as in great.

What, then, would the individuals composing a nation have to sacrifice in the way of personal interest in the event of international legislation taking place? Neither money nor liberty, neither pleasure nor comfort! At the most, they would have to repress a certain brute ferocity, which exists in most people, and which occasionally urges them to rebel against civilization and morality, and to join the wild beasts in satisfying their desire for possession or vengeance at any cost. But these desires do not frequently obsess a nation, and restraint at such a time would generally be acknowledged gratefully after the crisis had passed. Looking forward to such possibilities in cold blood, it is no sacrifice to provide against them; still less is it a sacrifice to provide against the possible running *amuck* of other nations.

As to the positive advantages, the "adequate inducement in the shape of personal interest" offered by the system in question, it is hoped that every preceding chapter will have demonstrated that *no one* could fail to reap the advantages; that nothing but abnormal stupidity could leave the inducements unrecognized. Its adoption would mean the further security of liberty, the further protection of rights.

It has been shown that the humblest individual in a nation is directly affected by its foreign relations; more than that, that strife between distant countries may affect his personal interests disastrously—that, in short, interdependence is not an hypothesis, but is a living reality.

So the humblest individual is concerned in the security of commerce, the safeguarding of food supplies, the lessening of taxation, the better insurance against the losses, financial and mortal, entailed by war—war with its horrors of famine, fire, pestilence, and rape, even apart from its bloodshed. He is concerned in these things not only for his own sake, but for the sake of those who are near and dear to him. And he must surely see that international legislation would protect and benefit him in all these several ways; that it is the *right* thing, the next step to be taken in the evolution of civilized nations, which means that, once taken, it would redound to his own happiness, to the happiness of his countrymen, and to that of the world as a whole.

Perhaps he will see yet deeper; perhaps he will see that it is in the heart and soul of things that this thing shall be done; and perhaps in the silence of his own heart he will hear himself saying,— Yes, we *are* dependent upon each other; we are not separate. Nor do I care how this thing may benefit me. It will benefit my country and every member of the human race. It is the inevitable outcome of evolution; it is a step to be taken; and it will be necessary for but two or three nations to take it together to make it an accomplished fact. And I will work to help it forward, will work for the freedom, the protection, the happiness of men and women and children who need my help. This way I can help them in the mass, enduringly. A new initiative is needed to give strength and hope to the nations; and the Will of the people must be aroused from its slumber of years. I will do my part in arousing that giant Will, by word and deed, that the initiative may be given for which the people wait. I, cost what it may, will see what one man can do among millions, how an infinitesimal part can affect the whole to its remotest borders, so that among races yet unborn there may be less of suffering and sorrow, more of happiness and peace.

So, perhaps, some will find themselves thinking. They may do as much and more than they think. But to many it will scarcely occur that they, so insignificant, can do more than contribute a vague and general approval, supposing that they go so far as that.

This is one of the great barriers to the further evolution of the race: that individuals do not believe in and therefore cannot exercise their own power. "What is one among so many?"—the universal excuse for inaction, for knock-kneed and degrading ineptitude. The world may be said to re-

CONCLUSION. 149

volve on an atom: is man less than an atom? Too often he acts as if he thought so, refusing to believe that he has any actual voice in the government of his own country, still less in the destinies of foreign states.

Man continually forgets that he occupies the proud position of being called a Man, and perhaps does not know that this word is derived from a Sanscrit root which means *to think*. Whether he happens to know this or not, he stands in constant danger of passing a most inglorious existence. His sense of responsibility is dormant; but, worst of all, he does not believe in himself. Man's greatest sin to-day is his lack of faith in man.

Sometimes he claims to believe that God made him in His own image and breathed into him the breath of life—the same breath of fire and power that brought the worlds into being. With this belief too lightly attached to the outskirts of his consciousness, he says, "What am I among so many?" An abortion, God might have to answer; make the best of yourself at that! And if he likes to classify himself among the abortions, he must be left there till a merciful Providence removes him. But if not, then let him arise and claim his birthright, let him exercise his divine powers, let him make his voice heard and his deeds speak among the people who are his companions on life's pilgrimage.

Sometimes, on the other hand, he claims to be the product of millions of years of evolution,—he, a man, the flower of it all. Are the labours of æons to result in this puerile cry, "What am I among so many?" Is the struggle for existence to leave him a thing without power, part of the refuse left by the wayside on the world's grand march? Would he revert to the protoplasmic mass from which he believes he came? If not, let him remember that inactivity means loss of function, and that if he would preserve his powers he must use them.

Sometimes he claims to be the exfoliation of a universal divine Spirit, itself the container of all potencies; that he is a miniature of the universe around him, with lightnings playing through his body, with thoughts in his mind that are the thoughts of the soul of Nature. Must he, believing that there exist within himself illimitable and undreamed-of possibilities, join with others in their feeble cry, and thus belittle his own origin and resist his own destiny? If not, let him work with the gods for the upbuilding of the future.

Whichever way he may think, let him act accordingly; let him be true to his belief and to himself; let him remember that he has duties as well as rights.

A dozen determined men, believing in themselves and their mission, can mould the thought of the age in which they live. One man has done it before now. Four men revolutionized the thought of the English-speaking world in less than a quarter of a century. These may be exceptional cases, both of men and of missions, but the humblest and least of men, able to make one simple fact his own, must come in time to understand that he and his fact between them may constitute a world-moving power; and when not only the men and the thought are ready, but the time is ripe for the doing of the deed, then nothing can withstand a movement which great nature has made her own.

. . . . .

Whether the conclusions put forward in this brochure be approved or disapproved, they should not be devoid of interest, if only because they will be made national political issues in most of the leading European countries and in the United States of America within the next few years.

This may seem an idle boast and an empty prophecy; but nothing could be gained by deliberately forecasting such an event if overwhelming probability did not point to its occurrence.

There has been in existence for some time past a

private body, with a membership scattered throughout the world, working to bring this about. The members of this organization will not reveal their connection with it, but those who know them know that their influence is sufficient to guarantee that the matter shall be submitted to the people.

"To every thing there is a season, and a time to every purpose under the heaven . . . a time to keep silence, and a time to speak." Ten years ago no public step of this sort could have been taken advantageously, but such rapid strides have been made since then in the lives of nations that conditions are at last ripe for a far-reaching propaganda.

As success in these issues depends upon the action of people in the mass, it is to the people of every class and race that this preliminary appeal is made, that they may use their power and insist that principles of right shall govern the councils of nations, and that an International Convention shall be called to consider how this may best be done.[1]

[1] See Note H., on "The English-Speaking Peoples"; see also at the end of this volume an Addendum in regard to the communication of August 27th, 1898, from the Czar of Russia to the Powers.

NOTES.

NOTE A.
(From p. 40.)

A NATION AN ORGANISM.

THE views of Mr. Herbert Spencer on this subject have been admirably summarized by Mr. Howard Collins in his *Epitome of the Synthetic Philosophy*, pp. 389 to 391. Dealing with the Inductions of Sociology, under the heading "What is a Nation?", Mr. Collins says:

"212. A society is an entity; for, though formed of discrete units, a certain concreteness in the aggregate of them is implied by the general persistence of the arrangements among them throughout the area occupied.

"213. The attributes of a society being like those of a living body, the reasons have now to be considered for asserting that the permanent relations among the parts of a society, are analogous to the permanent relations among the parts of a living body."

Under the heading "A Society is an Organism," the author continues:

"214. The first trait for regarding a society as an organism, is that it undergoes continuous growth.

"215. As a society grows, its parts become unlike: it exhibits increase of structure.

"216. This community will be more fully appreciated on observing that progressive differentiation of social structures is accompanied by progressive differentiation of social functions.

"217. The functions are not simply different, but their differences are so related as to make one another possible. This reciprocal aid causes mutual dependence of the parts. And the mutually-dependent parts, living by and for one another, form an aggregate constituted on the same general principle as is an individual organism. In respect of the 'physiological division of labour' a social organism and an individual organism are entirely alike.

"218. How the combined actions of mutually-dependent parts constitute life of the whole, and how there hence results a parallelism between social life and animal life, we see still more clearly on learning that the life of every visible organism is constituted by the lives of units too minute to be seen by the unaided eye. On seeing this, there is less difficulty in regarding a nation of human beings as an organism.

"219. The relation between the lives of the units and the life of the aggregate has a further character common to the two cases. By a catastrophe the life of the aggregate may be destroyed without immediately destroying the lives of all its units;

while, on the other hand, if no catastrophe abridges it, the life of the aggregate is far longer than the lives of its units.

"The life of the whole is quite unlike the lives of the units; though it is a life produced by them."

[This last statement is true only when the "units" are simple cells, and even then more recent investigations have proved that unicellular organisms are creatures of far greater complexity than was formerly supposed.]

"220. From these likenesses between the social organism and the individual organism, we must turn to an extreme unlikeness. The parts of an animal form a concrete whole; but the parts of a society form a whole which is discrete. While the living units composing the one are bound together in close contact, the living units composing the other are free, are not in contact, and are more or less widely dispersed."

[At the time when Mr. Herbert Spencer wrote his *Principles of Sociology*, physiological science may have held that the living units composing an animal form were "bound together in close contact," but modern experts entertain views which would have enabled Mr. Spencer to draw a comparison here as elsewhere, instead of noting an apparent difference. Professor E. J. Marey, for instance, in his *Animal Mechanism* (p. 9), said years ago that "From the invisible atom to the celestial body lost in space, everything is subject to motion. Everything gravitates in an immense or in an infinitely little orbit. *Kept at a definite distance one from the other*, in proportion to the motion which animates them, the molecules present constant relations, which they lose only by the addition or the subtraction of a certain quantity of motion." From which it would follow that the living units composing an animal organism are *not* in contact, and are, relatively speaking, as free as the units composing a society.]

"221. How, then, can there be any parallelism?" —continues the author of the *Epitome*, arguing, in this respect, on an erroneous supposition. "Though discrete instead of concrete (?), the social aggregate is rendered a living whole by emotional and intellectual language; it is by this agency that the mutual dependence of parts which constitutes organization is effectually established.

"222. We now arrive at a cardinal difference in the two kinds of organisms. In the one, consciousness is concentrated in a small part of the aggregate. In the other, it is diffused throughout the aggregate: all the units possess the capacities for happiness and misery in approximately equal degrees. As there is no social sensorium, the welfare of the aggregate, considered apart from that of the units, is not an end to be sought."

This "cardinal difference," in the light of recent science, ceases to be a difference, and could, in fact, be adduced as a further and particularly striking parallelism. For consciousness in the animal organism is *not* "concentrated in a small part of the aggregate." On the contrary, it is diffused throughout the aggregate. In his *Elements of Physiological Psychology* (Part II, chap. x., § 21), Professor G. T. Ladd states that:

"No good ground exists for speaking of any special organ or seat of memory. Every organ—indeed, every area and every element—of the nervous system *has its own memory.*" And in § 4 of the same chapter the Professor shows that "there is no special organ of will."

Some physiologists prefer to use the word "irritability," when speaking of micro-organisms, in the place of the word "consciousness"; but this is largely a question of terminology, for irritability implies sensation, and sensation is inconceivable apart from consciousness. "Affinity," again, is sometimes used to account for motion apart from consciousness; but it would be difficult to exclude some elementary form of desire from the idea of affinity.

In *The Psychic Life of Micro-Organisms*, by Alfred Binet, some valuable information is given in regard to this subject, all of which goes to prove that consciousness in the animal organism is diffused throughout the aggregate, not only as stated by Professor Ladd—in the sense that every organ has a consciousness of its own—but to the extent of demonstrating that such seemingly automatic processes as those of digestion, assimilation, and so forth are the result of the action of micro-organisms which perform their function with as much deliberation as is found among ants, not to mention certain human beings.

M. Binet says in his Preface to the American edition (p. iv.):

"The more closely the phenomena of life are scrutinized, and the more carefully they are studied in their various aspects, the more certain does the conclusion become that the processes attributed to physico-chemical forces in reality obey much more complicated laws. To illustrate, it was at one time conceded that the phenomena of resorption and nutrition were explainable by diffusion and endosmosis; Dutrochet, upon his discovery of endosmosis, imagined even that he had discovered the principle of life. At the present time we know that the walls of the intestines do not in any wise act like the inanimate membrane used in experiments in endosmosis. They are covered with epithelial cells, each of which is an organism endowed with a complex of properties. The protoplasm of these cells lays hold of food by an act of prehension, exactly as the ciliate Infusoria and other unicellular organisms do, that lead an independent life. In the intestines of cold-blooded animals the cells emit prolongations which seize the minute drops of fatty matter and, carrying them into the protoplasm of the cell, convey them thence into the chylifactive ducts. There is still another mode of absorption of fatty matters, met with among cold-blooded as well as warm-blooded animals: the lymphatic cells pass out from the adenoid tissue which contains them, so that upon arriving at the surface of the intestines they seize the particles of fatty matter there present and, laden with their prey, make their way back to the lymphatics.

"Accordingly, the faculty of seizing food and of exercising a choice among foods of different kinds—a property essentially psychological—appertains to the anatomical elements of the tissues, just as it does to all unicellular beings, in the manner shown in our treatise. It is plainly impossible to explain these facts by the introduction of physico-chemical forces. They are the essential phenomena of life and are the exclusive appurtenance of living protoplasm.

"If the existence of psychological phenomena in lower organisms is denied, it will be necessary to assume that these phenomena can be superadded in the course of evolution, in proportion as an organism grows more perfect and complex. Nothing could be more inconsistent with the teachings of general physiology, which shows us that all vital phenomena are previously present in non-differentiated cells."

The past twenty years have witnessed enormous strides in the development of microscopy, and every discovery thus made in regard to the constitution of the human organism has emphasized the fact that it is a "society," and that to know the laws governing the physical growth of an individual, is to know the laws governing the physical growth of a nation. The process of the mental and moral growth of both nations and individuals is still more evidently identical.

NOTE B.
(From p. 45.)
UNSELFISHNESS.

THE question of motive is not emphasized in these pages because it is not essential to the main argument nor to the conclusions presented. No one will deny the importance of right motive. "Enlightened selfishness," from one point of view, is a contradiction in terms, and those who use the phrase in a philosophical sense must be left to defend it as best they can.

Quite apart from the mental and moral effects of wrong motive, selfishness, in the ordinary sense of the word, must disastrously affect the *quality* of an action, even though it may not affect its direction. As Emerson says in his essay on *Experience*, "The sentiment from which it sprung determines the dignity of any deed, and the question ever is, not, what you have done or forborne, but, at whose command you have done or forborne it."

Yet, as we cannot always hope for both right motive and right action, it is better to have right action and wrong or mixed motive, than the action and the motive alike wrong. The continual performance of right actions induces right motive in time.

Spontaneous unselfishness is a higher development than mere right conduct. In a passage in Mr. Herbert Spencer's *Principles of Ethics*, "spontaneous efforts to further the welfare of others" are stated to be the result of the evolution of conduct. When a man habitually does the unselfish thing, without calculation, he has then, and then only, become an ideally moral mân.

But although unselfish motive is frequently met with in individuals, and right conduct still more frequently, it is as yet early in the evolution of nations to expect more than rare outbursts of real unselfishness. One must agree with Professor Sidgwick (*Practical Ethics*, p. 11): "When J. S. Mill says, in the peroration of a powerful address, 'I do not attempt to stimulate you with the prospect of direct rewards, either earthly or heavenly; the less we think about being rewarded in either way the better for us,' I think it is a hard saying, too hard for human nature. The demand that happiness shall be connected with virtue cannot be finally quelled in this way"—at least not so far as the international aspect of the problem is concerned; which does not alter the fact that although Mill's saying was "hard," it was none the less true.

Selfishness springs from what has been called "the great heresy of separateness." It is an attempt to ignore humanity's fundamental unity of interest; to isolate the unit in the midst of the mass. The impossibility of doing this and the fatuity of attempting it, are shown in a later Note.

NOTE C.
(From p. 49.)

THE MORALITY OF THE EVOLUTIONARY PROCESS.

MR. HERBERT SPENCER, in an article entitled "Evolutionary Ethics," in *Appleton's Popular Science Monthly* for February, 1898, commenting upon Professor Huxley's Romanes Lecture, defends himself against "that brutal individualism which some persons ascribe" to him.

"In a chapter of the *Principles of Ethics* entitled 'Altruism versus Egoism,' it is contended that from the dawn of life altruism of a kind (parental altruism) has been as essential as egoism; and that in the associated state the function of altruism becomes wider, and the importance of it greater, in proportion as the civilization becomes higher. . . . Everywhere it is asserted that the process of adaptation (which, in its direct and indirect forms, is a part of the cosmic process) must continuously tend (under peaceful conditions) to produce a type of society and a type of individual in which 'the instincts of savagery in civilized men' will be not only 'curbed,' but repressed. And I believe that in few, if any, writings will be found as unceasing a denunciation of that brute form of the struggle for existence which has been going on between societies, and which, though in early times a cause of progress, is now becoming a cause of retrogression."

Mr. Spencer then cites the following significant paragraphs from his *Principles of Ethics:*

"The limit of evolution of conduct is consequently not reached until, beyond avoidance of direct and indirect injuries to others, there are spontaneous efforts to further the welfare of others."

"It may be shown that the form of nature which thus to justice adds beneficence, is one which adaptation to the social state produces."—§ 54.

NOTE D.

(From p. 58.)

'SPLENDID ISOLATION,' OR THE INTERDEPENDENCE OF NATIONS.

A MODIFIED form of this opposition to the international application of sound principle, is to be found in the "splendid isolation" theory, which is becoming the curse of the British and American nations. As a policy it may be accounted for, in part, as a praiseworthy reaction from the system of "association for purposes of plunder" which has so often prevailed in the past when nations have combined for "purposes of defence." But fundamentally, the theory is based upon the supposition that the interests of nations are antagonistic and that isolation is a means of self-preservation.

This supposition is absolutely opposed to every known fact, as stated in Chapter IV. Its falsity has been proved by actual experiment in the case of China, for China's position in relation to foreign powers is due to her internal disorganization, which has been brought about to a great extent by her long-continued attempts to cut herself off from the rest of the world. In her case we see the "splendid isolation" theory carried to its logical extreme. Japan would have been in the same condition that

China is in to-day if she had persisted in her early policy.

One has only to turn to nature to get proof positive of the interdependence of all her component parts, nations included. This fact is admitted and exemplified by jurists, as is shown in the following quotation from an article by J. M. Irvine on "International Law" in *Chambers' Encyclopædia*—corroboration of value, seeing that it is the business of writers in Encyclopædias to be conservative in their statements:

"The fundamental conception of international jurisprudence is that of the interdependence of states, as opposed to their independence. The fact of the reality of such interdependence is every day becoming clearer with the increase of complexity in the social, commercial, and political ties by which the nations of the world are bound one to another. No state, for example, can administer its own criminal law or execute its own criminal judgments without the continual aid of all other states; and in declaring at its Oxford meeting in 1880 that extradition might take place at all times independently of any contractual obligations, or, in other words, that the right of extradition is a right at common law, the Institute of International Law formally accepted the doctrine of the interdependence of states as a conception fundamental in the law of nations."

In America the isolation theory has grown up in consequence of the advice contained in Washington's celebrated Farewell Address, advice which, given to the American people at the close of the eighteenth century, when the Republic was still in its infancy, is made to do service to-day, when the nation has for long been adult. Furthermore, the meaning of the Address has been grievously misinterpreted.

This was convincingly demonstrated by Mr. Richard Olney, Secretary of State during Mr. Cleveland's second administration, in an address delivered at Harvard, and afterwards published in *The Atlantic Monthly* for May, 1898, under the title "International Isolation of the United States." In it he said:

"The Washington rule of isolation, then, proves on examination to have a much narrower scope than the generally accepted versions give to it. Those versions of it may and undoubtedly do find countenance in loose and general and unconsidered statements of public men both of the Washington era and of later times. Nevertheless it is the rule of Washington, and not that of any other man or men, that is authoritative with the American people, so that the inquiry what were Washington's reasons for the rule and how far those reasons are applicable to the facts of the present day is both pertinent and important.

"Washington states his reasons with singular clearness and force. 'This nation,' he says in substance, 'is young and weak. Its remote and detached geographical situation exempts it from any necessary or natural connection with the ordinary politics or quarrels of European states. Let it therefore stand aloof from such politics and such quarrels and avoid any alliances that might connect it with them. This the nation should do that it may gain time—that the country may have peace during such period as is necessary to enable it to settle and mature its institutions and to reach without interruption that degree of strength and consistency which will give it the command of its own fortunes.'

"Such is the whole theory of the Washington rule of isolation. Its simple statement shows that the considerations justifying the rule to his mind can no longer be urged in support of it. Time has been gained—our institutions are proven to have a stability and to work with a success exceeding all expectation—and though the nation is still young, it has long since ceased to be feeble or to lack the power to command its own fortunes.

"It is just as true that the achievements of modern science have annihilated the time and space that once separated the Old World from the New. In these days of telephones and railroads and ocean cables and ocean steamships, it is difficult to realize that Washington could write to the French Ambassador at London in 1790, 'We at this great distance from the northern parts of Europe hear of wars and rumors of wars as if they were the events or reports of another planet.'"

Mr. Olney touches but lightly on the "Monroe

Doctrine," as much misunderstood in its way as is the rule laid down by Washington.

"The United States is certainly now entitled to rank among the great Powers of the world. Yet, while its place among the nations is assured, it purposely takes its stand outside the European family circle to which it belongs, and neither accepts the responsibilities of its place nor secures its advantages. It avowedly restricts its activities to the American continents and intentionally assumes an attitude of absolute aloofness from everything outside those continents. This rule of policy is not infrequently associated with another which is known as the Monroe doctrine—as if the former grew out of the Monroe doctrine, or were, in a sense, a kind of consideration for that doctrine, or a sort of compliment to it. In reality the rule of isolation originated and was applied many years before the Monroe doctrine was proclaimed. No doubt that consistency requires that the conduct toward America which America expects of Europe should be observed by America toward Europe. Nor is there any more doubt that such reciprocal conduct is required of us not only by consistency but by both principle and expediency. The vital feature of the Monroe doctrine is that no European Power shall forcibly possess itself of American soil and forcibly control the political fortunes and destinies of its people. Assuredly America can have no difficulty in governing its behavior toward Europe on the same lines."

Distorting the Monroe doctrine and pushing the application of Washington's rule to a point that would have been ridiculous even in his own time, can have but one result. "Do we want the Armenian butcheries stopped? To any power that will send its fleet through the Dardanelles and knock the Sultan's palace about his ears, we boldly tender our 'moral support.' Do we want the same rights and facilities of trade in Chinese ports and territory that are accorded to the people of any other country? We loudly hark Great Britain on to the task of achieving that result, but come to the rescue ourselves with not a gun, nor a man, nor a ship, with nothing but our 'moral support.' . . . Does a foreign question or controversy present itself appealing however forcibly to our sympathies or sense of right—what happens the moment it is suggested that the United States should seriously participate in its settlement? A shiver runs through all the ranks of capital lest the uninterrupted course of money-making be interfered with; the cry of 'Jingo!' comes up in various quarters; advocates of peace at any price make themselves heard from innumerable pulpits and rostrums; while practical politicians invoke the doctrine of the Farewell Address as an absolute bar to all positive action. The upshot is more or less explosions of sympathy at more or less public meetings, and, if the case is a very strong one, a more or less tardy tender by the government of its 'moral support.'

"Is that a creditable part for a great nation to play in the affairs of the world? . . . Isolation that is nothing but a shirking of the responsibilities of high place and great power is simply ignominious."

In terms of dollars and cents, how can the United States be 'independent' of other countries when in 1896, taking that as an average year, over 27 per cent. of all the wheat it produced was exported; when over 43 per cent. of the mineral oil it produced was exported; when 65 per cent. of the cotton it produced was exported?

The total domestic exports from the United States during the fiscal year ending June, 1897, excluding specie, amounted to $1,032,007,603 or about £205,000,000; over 46.3 per cent. of which were sent to Great Britain and Ireland alone, and over 57.2 per cent. of which were sent to Great Britain, Ireland, and the Colonies and Dependencies.

During the same period the value of the merchandise imported into the United States amounted to $764,730,412 or about £153,000,000; over 21.9 per cent. of which came from Great Britain and Ireland alone, while 33.5 per cent. came from Great Britain, Ireland, and the Colonies and Dependencies. (*Statistics*, Treasury Department, U. S. A.)

These figures must surely upset the isolation theory and the notion that the United States is independent of foreign relationships. A merchant is dependent upon his customers. Their welfare benefits him. In the same way he is dependent upon those from whom he buys, their stability and general reliability being of great consequence to him, just as the constant provision of raw material is a matter of great consequence to the manufacturer. They are all of them interdependent.

The same blight of imagined independence has fallen upon Great Britain; and if to a lesser extent than upon the United States, there is certainly less excuse for it in the former case than can be put forward on behalf of the American Commonwealth. Great Britain is a huge trader, and from many other points of view there is hardly a country on the inhabited globe with which she is not directly connected by bonds of mutual interest.

During the fiscal year 1894 to 1895, Great Britain and Ireland did trading to the amount of £690,559,507 or about $3,450,000,000—£446,922,574 or about $2,200,000,000 of this being Imports, and £243,636,933 or about $1,200,000,000 being Exports.

The United Kingdom, India, and the Colonies together, during the same period, traded to the extent of £1,100,461,968 or about $5,500,000,000; carrying a total debt of £1,099,369,556, or about $5,400,000,000. (*The Statesman's Year Book*, 1896.) What a large percentage of this trade is carried on with the United States has already been shown.

Can the much-vaunting practical person still deny that nations are interdependent? Hardly, it would seem; yet whenever mention is made of foreign alliances he bristles with indignation at the idea of Great Britain, for instance, involving herself by mixing her own interests with those of some other nation—as if her interests could possibly be more mixed than they are already. His indignation may be due to his dreadfully limited outlook.

Incapable of seeing anything beyond what he deems a necessary *quid pro quo* of dollars and cents, he insists upon considering an alliance as a business partnership, demanding to know how much money, or how many ships, guns, and men, some nation is at once ready to put into the concern. Even from that point of view his outlook is too confined to enable him to estimate prospects: the money, the ships, the guns, the men, must be ready to jump into the scales before he would seriously contemplate an alliance; and for fear that he might have to give something in return for what he gets, and that he might not be able to employ his increased capital immediately, he prefers to "wait until the crisis arrives."

If it is suggested that the nation in question may not care to enter into an alliance with him and his fellows, on such a basis, in a time of crisis, he replies that Great Britain is rich enough to buy allies whenever she needs them, and if that nation cannot be bought, others can be!

Atavism and its products are disagreeable, though unavoidable: are sometimes more than disagreeable, occasionally manifesting a shameful and degrading perversion of every better instinct.

Rome, among other nations, had a rather bitter experience with mercenaries; England may pass through the same experience too, if she insists upon it, though it is to be hoped, for her sake, that the experience she has had already of hired allies will prevent further lapses in that direction. But,

> "O queen from of old of the seas,
> England, art thou of them too
> That drink of the poisonous flood,
> That hide under poisonous trees?"

Is this to be the outcome of all her struggles, of all her efforts toward higher and better things? Must she depend at the last upon mercenaries, upon hirelings—and fall as Rome fell? There will be no such necessity, if she will rely upon her own native strength and will use that, while recognizing the interdependence of nations and the wisdom of acting upon principle.

Those who regard an alliance as necessarily partaking of the nature of a business partnership, overlook their own every-day experience. It would almost seem that they cannot conceive of association for any other purpose than that of *direct* financial gain; yet Trades Unions, Employers' Protective Associations, Clubs, Societies with political, legal, scientific, literary, philanthropic, and other objects, are all common examples of association for other purposes than that of direct gain. Poor men as well as rich may belong to them, being well qualified for reasons quite other than financial, the poor men being sometimes the most useful members of the organization.

Representative government itself is an important instance of association for the purpose of mutual benefit, without direct gain and on payment of a more or less heavy price. The enactment of laws by such a government is another example of mutual agreement for the benefit of all concerned, though these laws may limit the liberties of the individuals enacting them.

On an international scale there are many illustrations of the same kind of association, one of which, indirectly commercial though it is, is that of the Universal Postal Union; another, purely humanitarian in its objects, is that of the agreement entered into at the Convention of Geneva of 1864.

It is impossible for a nation to isolate itself, and the only question is, to what extent it cares to affiliate with another or other nations in order to promote the interests they share in common, many of which are generally admitted to be superior to the directly commercial interests, however important the latter may be.

Much has been said recently concerning an Anglo-American Alliance, and the usual objections have been raised on both sides of the Atlantic on the score of doubtful *quid pro quo*, this way and that. But if such an alliance were entered into on the basis of self-interest only, or, on the other hand, on merely sentimental grounds, it would do more harm than good; it would become a danger instead of a blessing to the world.

Mutual self-interest is a bond of the flimsiest description, liable to snap at any moment as conditions change. Commercial partnerships conducted on a strictly business basis are not only frequently impermanent—proverbially so when the parties to them are incessantly looking for *quid pro quo*—but, once broken, lead to a bitterness of opposition that is not met with among ordinarily competing firms.

Such an alliance, then, to be enduring, would have to be *based upon something which would not change in itself*, as sentiment and self-interest change. Ties of language, religion, race, are not sufficient by themselves. Common recognition of principle and mutual agreement as to its practical application, would alone supply the basis that is needed.

Perhaps Mr. Arthur Balfour, speaking as a member of the Marquess of Salisbury's cabinet, suggested the only true foundation for an association of the kind, though he made no practical proposal for the application of the principle he enunciated.

" We have a domestic patriotism," he said, " as Scotchmen or Englishmen or as Irishmen, or what you will, we have an Imperial patriotism as citizens of the British Empire [or an American patriotism as citizens of the great Republic]; but surely, in addition to that, we have also an Anglo-Saxon patriotism ["Anglo-Celtic" was suggested by Dr. Conan Doyle] which embraces within its ample folds the whole of that great race which has done so much in every branch of human effort, and in that branch of human effort which has produced free institutions and free communities.

"We may be taxed with being idealists and dreamers in this matter. I would rather be an idealist and a dreamer, and I look forward with confidence to the time when our ideals will have become real and our dreams will be embodied in actual political fact. For, after all, circumstances will tend in that direction in which we look.

"It cannot but be that those who share our language, our literature, our laws, our religion, everything that makes a nation great, and who share in substance our institutions—it cannot but be that *the time will come when they will feel that they and we have a common duty to perform, a common office to fulfil among the nations of the world.*"

Mr. Olney struck the same keynote in concluding his Harvard address. Referring to the close community existing between the British and American peoples, "in origin, speech, thought, literature, institutions, ideals—in the kind and degree of civilization enjoyed by both," he added:

"In that same community, and *in that co-operation in good works which should result from it*, lies, it is not too much to say, the best hope for the future not only of the two kindred peoples but of the human race itself."

An alliance based upon principles of freedom, of justice, of responsibility, would not be as *against* any other nation or combination of nations, but largely *for* them all. A door would be left wide open by which other nations would be welcomed as sharers in the benefits accruing from such an association; and, as the years passed, we might live to hear less of "America for the Americans," less of "Britain for the British," proclaiming, as such cries do, the very epitome of selfishness; we might live to hear a different cry—"An alliance of Nations to maintain justice in the world."

A difficulty lies in finding a practical basis for such an alliance, in regard to which more will be found in Part IV.

NOTE E.
(From p. 73.)
CHRISTIANITY.

IN this and in the preceding chapter, particular stress has been laid upon the views of Mr. Herbert Spencer and Professor Huxley, because they are commonly though erroneously supposed to be supporters of an individualism which is interpreted by those whom it suits to so interpret it as an excuse for a short-sighted selfishness. Many people who wish to obtain some immediate advantage at the sacrifice of principle defend their conduct on the ground that selfishness is necessary in an age of competition, and that consideration for others is unpractical and sentimental.

No scientist would adopt or condone such a ridiculously unscientific attitude, but those who do, will often claim that "Science" supports them, with its theory of "the survival of the fittest" and so forth; and "Science" is supposed by such people to be synonymous with Professor Huxley and Mr. Spencer. Hence the importance of adducing their views as one more nail in the coffin of ignorant, self-destructive, but self-parading selfishness.

If opposition to the views put forward cannot come from scientific sources; if, on the contrary, modern science as a whole is one concentrated argument in support of an enlightened altruism as binding upon the individual, the community, and the nation, and if evolution demands the fulfilment of duties to others, opposition need hardly be expected from any other quarter. It is difficult to believe that any one calling himself a Christian and adopting the teachings of the *New Testament*, would show himself less true to principle and less consistent with his own ethical system, than are those who do not claim to be followers of the gentle Jesus.

So it is taken for granted throughout these pages that those who are really believers in Christ's teachings, as distinguished from " professing Christians," must recognize the need for Christian practice as between the nations, as well as between individuals. They need only ask themselves, What would Christ say in regard to this matter?

It has been remarked many times that some exponents of religion, at the first outbreak of international hostilities, assume a new character the very opposite of the function with which they usually expect to be credited, busying themselves with prayers to propitiate the god of battles, and succeeding, maybe, in adding a fanatical belief in the exclusive righteousness of their own cause to the natural fury of the combatants.

If this is true of the past, and of certain exponents of religion, it is to be hoped that the future will witness some atonement for such a monstrous perversion of Christianity; for the influence of the more enlightened section of the religious community should not only restrain such outbursts of barbarism in the event of war, but should hasten to encourage and support any rational proposal likely to promote peace.

NOTE F.
(From p. 109.)

THE INTERNATIONAL MARINE CONFERENCE.

"HALF a century ago, as it is well known, there did not exist any written law or regulation for the prevention of collisions between ships at sea. There was then only a general custom of the sea."

In January, 1863, England and France concluded agreements as to common rules, which they were by then forced to do, owing to their mutual interests in the navigation of the Channel. After much delay, and after these preliminary rules had been adopted by most civilized states, an International Conference was held at Washington in 1889, which was reported to the President of the United States by Mr. James G. Blaine, writing from the Department of State on February 12th, 1890, as follows:

"*To the President:*

"In pursuance to the provisions of the act of Congress approved July 9, 1888, an invitation was extended to the maritime powers to take part in a conference to be held at Washington, the objects of which were to revise and amend the rules, regulations, and practice concerning vessels at sea and navigation generally; to adopt a uniform system of marine signals, especially with reference to signaling in fog; to compare and discuss the various systems employed for the saving of life and property from shipwreck; to devise methods of reporting, marking, and removing dangerous wrecks and obstructions to navigation, and to establish uniform means of conveying to mariners warnings of storms and other information.

"Of the thirty-seven maritime powers invited, favorable responses to the invitation were received from twenty-seven, which included the principal nations. The delegates from the accepting powers met on the 16th of October last, and the International Marine Conference was organized.

"After a very satisfactory session, the Conference was finally concluded December 31, 1889. . . . Respectfully submitted."

The following powers were represented: Austria-Hungary, Belgium, Brazil, Chili, China, Costa Rica, Denmark, France, Germany, Great Britain, Guatemala, Hawaii, Honduras, Italy, Japan, Mexico, Netherlands, Nicaragua, Norway, Portugal, Russia, Siam, Spain, Sweden, Turkey, Uruguay, Venezuela, and the United States. (See the *Official Report* for the above.)

The quotation with which this Note opens, is taken from a Memorandum prepared by the Committee of the Second Northern Maritime Conference (representing a merchant fleet of over 2,000,000 tons register), held at Copenhagen, September,

1888, under the chairmanship of Mr. C. F. Tietgen, Chairman of the Copenhagen Chamber of Commerce.

In the same Memorandum, which contained suggestions to be submitted at the Washington Conference, the Committee of business men who drew it up declared that "it ought not to be forgotten that the realization of this plan aims at something more than the satisfaction of the behoof of the material interests; for it is through progress of this kind that the way shall be paved for a better mutual understanding between the nations, for better relations between them, and for a better comprehension of the truth that all the peoples of the earth, in spite of their national peculiarities, have got by Providence a common work to do and a common aim to strive for—*the development of the whole of mankind to a life in peace and harmony.*"

NOTE G.
(From p. 135.)
SULLY AND KANT.

IT will be remembered that the "Great Design" of Henry IV. of France and Elizabeth of England, as it is presented in Sully's *Memoirs*, though it contemplated the establishment of a General Council, representing all the states of Europe, was to have been a most warlike and arbitrary measure— a scheme of universal conquest, in short, with the crippling of the house of Austria as a first preliminary. After this had been done, Europe was to have undergone a process of redistribution, and was to have been thereafter governed by "laws and ordinances" under the direction of the Council, which it was proposed to form on the model of the Amphictyonic Assembly of ancient Greece.

Countries were to have been summarily disposed of, in the event of their holding aloof from the enterprise. "Should the Grand Duke of Muscovy, or Czar of Russia, who is believed to be the ancient Khan of Scythia, refuse to enter into the association after it is proposed to him, he ought to be treated like the Sultan of Turkey, deprived of his possessions in Europe, and confined to Asia only. . . ." (*Memoirs of the Duke of Sully*, Bohn's ed., vol. iv., p. 236.)

Sully says that the princes joining the association, which he describes as a "military confederacy," "after they had conquered with it whatever they would not suffer any stranger should share with them in Europe, would have sought to join to it such parts of Asia as were most commodiously situated, and particularly the whole coast of Africa, which is too near to our own territories for us not to be frequently incommoded by it. The only precaution to be observed in regard to these additional countries would have been to form them into new kingdoms, declare them united with the rest of the Christian powers, and bestow them on different princes, carefully observing to exclude those who before bore rank among the sovereigns of Europe." (*Loc. cit.*, vol. iv., p. 238.)

At the time of Henry's death the plans for carrying out this scheme had been thoroughly matured, and a most powerful combination of the European states had been formed to give it effect. The support of the Pope had been obtained: it was proposed to give him temporal power; the plan also including the conversion of the continual wars among the princes of Europe "into a perpetual war against the Infidels."

But the real end in view was most commendable, and reflects infinite credit upon Henry and his minister, for it was "to save both himself and his neighbours those immense sums which the maintenance of so many thousand soldiers, so many fortified places, and so many military expenses require; to free them for ever from the fear of those bloody catastrophes so common in Europe; to procure them an uninterrupted repose; and finally, to unite them all in an indissoluble bond of security and friendship, after which they might live together like brethren. . . ." (*Loc. cit.*, vol. iv., p. 233.)

Although such ends are worthy of the highest praise, the means proposed for their attainment cannot be commended; for in spite of the immense ability displayed in preparing the plan of campaign, its designers did not allow for the inevitable consequences of arbitrary and unjust methods. They also failed to realize that they were not merely dealing with princes, but with peoples who were already beginning to assert their rights.

It is easy to criticize such a plan, however, in the light of later experience. For its day it was an extraordinary expression of the world's desire for peace and for the establishment of international law and order. The design is all the more remarkable because its chief promoters were the most successful practical statesmen of their time. Sully, in particular, has gained general recognition at the hands of historians for his ability and sound common sense; and on that account his opinion concerning the European situation is of value, seeing that it applies as fittingly to conditions as they now exist as to those prevailing in the beginning of the seventeenth century.

"I dare further maintain," he says, "that peace is the great and common interest of Europe. . . . When I consider Europe as composed of such civilized people, I cannot but be astonished that she still continues to be governed by principles so narrow, and customs so barbarous. What is the consequence of that profound policy of which she is so vain, other than her own continual laceration and ruin? War is the resource in all places, and upon all occasions; she knows no other way, or conceives no other expedients: it is the sole resource of the most inconsiderable sovereign, as well as of the greatest potentate. . . . Why must we always impose on ourselves the necessity of passing through war to arrive at peace? the attainment of which is the end of all wars, and is a plain proof that recourse is had to war only for want of a better expedient. Nevertheless, we have so effectually confounded this truth, that we seem to make peace only that we may again be able to make war." (*Loc. cit.*, vol. ii., p. 353.)

That is the view of a practical statesman. Philosophers have not been slow to arrive at the same general conclusions, and some of them have suggested remedies similar to the "Great Design" of Henry, avoiding for the most part, however, the strange contradiction in his plan, which aimed at establishing a Perpetual Peace and which yet provided for a "perpetual war against the Infidels."

NOTES. 191

Omitting minor instances—such as the proposals of the Abbé de St. Pierre and of Rousseau—the essay on *Perpetual Peace* by Kant, published in 1795, and his earlier essay on *The Natural Principle of the Political Order*, are well-known contributions to the literature on this subject.

Kant was too profound a thinker to fall into the error of supposing that peace could actually be made perpetual. He lays this down very clearly in his *Philosophy of Law:* "Perpetual Peace, which is the ultimate end of all the Right of Nations, becomes in fact an impracticable idea. The political principles, however, which aim at such an end, and which enjoin the formation of such unions among the States as may promote a continuous *approximation* to a Perpetual Peace, are not impracticable; they are as practicable as this approximation itself, which is a practical problem involving a duty, and founded upon the Right of individual men and States." (Hastie's translation, sect. 61.)

Kant presents a very powerful argument in favour of international legislation. His "Seventh Proposition" in *The Natural Principle of the Political Order* is that:

"The problem of the establishment of a perfect Civil Constitution is dependent on the problem of the regulation of the external relations between the States conformably to Law; and without the solution of this latter problem it cannot be solved."

"What avails it," he comments, "to labour at

the arrangement of a Commonwealth as a Civil Constitution regulated by law among individual men? The same unsociableness which forced men to it, becomes again the cause of each Commonwealth assuming the attitude of uncontrolled freedom in its external relations, that is, as one State in relation to other States; and consequently, any one State must expect from any other the same sort of evils as oppressed individual men and compelled them to enter into a Civil Union regulated by law. Nature has accordingly again used the unsociableness of men, and even of great societies and political bodies, her creatures of this kind, as a means to work out through their mutual Antagonism a condition of rest and security. She works through wars, through the strain of never relaxed preparation for them, and through the necessity which every state is at last compelled to feel within itself, even in the midst of peace, to begin some imperfect efforts to carry out her purpose. And, at last, after many devastations, overthrows, and even complete internal exhaustion of their powers, the nations are driven forward to the goal which Reason might have well impressed upon them, even without so much sad experience. This is none other than the advance out of the lawless state of savages and the entering into a Federation of Nations."

"The necessity in which men involve one another," he continues, "must compel the Nations to the very resolution—however hard it may appear—to which the savage in his uncivilized state, was so unwillingly compelled, when he had to surrender his brutal liberty and seek rest and security in a Constitution regulated by law." (Hastie's translation, pp. 16, 17.)

It is not often that statesmen and philosophers agree, and Sully, one of the greatest of European statesmen, and Kant, whom many have called the father of modern philosophy, agree in relation to this matter in so many important respects that their concurrence affords valuable testimony in support of the conclusions now submitted.

NOTE H.
(From p. 152.)
THE ENGLISH-SPEAKING PEOPLES.

Is it not for the English-speaking peoples to take the initiative in this matter? Is not this the only practical basis for the proposed alliance? The English-speaking peoples claim to be pre-eminently civilized. They are not a single race, but a heterogeneous mass of Anglo-Saxons, Celts, Dutch, Germans, Scandinavians, Latins, and of many other different elements, sharing, however, the same ideas and institutions.

Has not the time almost come when the United States and the United Kingdom and Colonies will feel, as Mr. Balfour said, that they have "a common duty to perform, a common office to fulfil among the nations of the world"?[1] The present is a magnificent opportunity. If it is not seized it may be a chance missed for ever, so far as existing nations are concerned.

Rome had a similar chance, not only as a single Empire, but when the Eastern and Western Empires were virtually as distinct as are the United

[1] See Note D., on "'Splendid Isolation,' or the Interdependence of Nations," of which this Note is practically a continuation.

States and Great Britain to-day. The rulers of the Latin-speaking peoples might have enacted international laws and made them binding wherever the Latin tongue was spoken. These laws would have affected surrounding nations, would probably have been acceded to by them also, and would thus have formed an imperishable system by which the relations of states could have been thereafter regulated. The Latin-speaking peoples missed their chance, paying for their lack of foresight with disintegration and a narrow escape from extinction. They relied upon brute strength, not upon justice.

Are miserable jealousies and trumpery policies to stand in the way of this saving achievement to-day? It is to be hoped not. The good sense of the people and their appreciation of right principles will surely prevail against separative forces, and the alliance, so much talked about, but for which, in the past, *no practical basis has been suggested*, will be entered into, not for purposes of offence, but by way of mutual consent to laws, to which all nations will be invited to accede, and from the establishment of which all the races of the earth will receive enduring benefit.

If there are any in America who, too blind to see that it would benefit their own country, can admit that it would benefit the rest of the world, and who yet say that the rest of the world is nothing to them for America is all in all—their love for their country should make them beware. Expansion is the first law of life; and though expansion of territory may not be necessary after a certain point, expansion of interest, of commerce, of thought, is. Otherwise expansive forces are hurled back upon themselves and congest: attacking some weak spot, some natural loophole for their repressed activities, they explode, and disintegration results.

Apart from such considerations, which would be utterly unworthy if all people realized their moral responsibilities, it is to be regretted that comparatively few Americans have any real faith in the power of their country as a leading factor in the elevation of the race. Individual Americans have the reputation in Europe of being braggarts: and there is some basis for the imputation. Yet it would be the greatest possible mistake to attribute the brag to conceit or to irrepressible self-confidence. A man who is really self-confident never brags; a man who is trying to be self-confident sometimes does.

If Americans were to believe, as they would be justified in believing, that in their country's possibilities lies the brightest hope for the future of the world, and that her influence on Europe is rapidly increasing and is already immense, they would talk less and do more, so that in a very short time America would take her place as one of the leaders if not the leader in the affairs of nations, instead of remaining, as she has usually done in the past, a spectator loudly vociferating from the top of a fence. To do this, in the way proposed, would not of necessity involve the increase of her army and navy by a man or a ship, for it would provide her with the middle course between the two extremes of isolation and aggressive acquisitiveness, and to follow either of these would oblige her to increase her armaments enormously.

It is possible that Great Britain realizes more clearly than the United States, both the dangers that beset her and her own inherent strength. She has had the longer and more varied experience of the two. In any case, it is almost certain that if the Government of the United States were to propose that a conference should be held to consider the question of International Law, the Government of the United Kingdom would cordially co-operate in the undertaking.

Only by joining an association of states, broadly based upon mutual consent to a system of federal law, can the union of Great Britain with her Colonies be permanently maintained.

At the present time Great Britain would be supported in her action by all the Colonies, though perhaps more on account of their loyalty to the mother-country and their friendly feeling for America, than because of their appreciation of the urgency of the question. The majority of the Colonies have had practically no experience of war, except with aboriginal races; they have had next to no experience in foreign affairs—the South African Colonies differing in these respects from the others.

It is difficult for a native of Adelaide, Melbourne, or Sydney, or of some up-country town such as Deniliquin, to contemplate seriously the always possible destruction of the British fleet, with all that that might involve. It is also difficult for a Londoner to understand that a fratricidal struggle between two such Colonies as Victoria and New South Wales is at least conceivable; yet the inhabitants of Melbourne and Sydney would frequently have been delighted in the past to have met "hand to hand," though in by no means a fraternal fashion. Popular feeling of that sort is liable to communicate itself to Governments; and as the Governments of Victoria and New South Wales are far more loosely connected than were those of Pennsylvania and South Carolina, for instance, in 1860, there is no knowing to what extremes antagonism might go. Tariff wars are the first step to wars of another sort.

With or without experience, however, the Colonists are unusually thoughtful people, and it is possible that they will be the first among the English-speaking communities to realize the vast importance of doing to-day that which may have become impracticable fifty years hence.

The mission of the English-speaking peoples as a whole, is not merely to exist; they have a higher and a nobler duty to perform. In the last century it fell to the lot of some of them to formulate and to give effect to a Declaration of Independence. In this century they have the opportunity to unite, and with others to formulate and to give effect to a Declaration of Interdependence. By taking advantage of existing conditions they can, at one stroke, safeguard their own interests and permanently benefit the world.

Addendum.

THE CZAR'S PLEA FOR PEACE.

THE CZAR'S PLEA FOR PEACE.

THIS little book was completed some time before the publication of the call by the Czar of Russia, through Count Muravieff, for an International Conference to "cement an agreement by a corporate consecration of the principles of equity and right, on which rest the security of States and the welfare of the peoples."

All that has been said herein will therefore be read in the additional light of that remarkable communication, which appeared in the Russian *Official Messenger* of August 27th, 1898. The communication has been translated as follows:

"The maintenance of general peace and the possible reduction of the excessive armaments which weigh upon all nations, present themselves to the whole world as an ideal toward which, in existing conditions, the endeavours of all Governments should be directed. The humanitarian and magnanimous ideas of his Majesty, the Emperor, my august master, have been won over to the view that this lofty aim is in conformity with the most essential interests and legitimate objects of all the powers; and the imperial Government thinks the present moment would be very favourable to seeking the means.

"International discussion is the most effectual way of insuring benefit to all peoples—by furthering a really durable peace; above all, by putting an end to the progressive development of the present armaments.

"In the course of the last twenty years the longing for general appeasement has grown especially pronounced in the consciences of civilized nations; and the preservation of peace has been put forward as an object of international policy. It is in its name that great States have concluded between themselves powerful alliances.

"It is the better to guarantee peace that they have developed in proportions hitherto unprecedented their military forces, and still continue to increase them, without shrinking from any sacrifice.

"Nevertheless, all these efforts have not yet been able to bring about the beneficent result desired—pacification.

"The financial charges following this growing tendency strike at the very root of public prosperity. The intellectual and physical strength of the nations' labour and capital are mostly diverted from their natural application, and are unproductively consumed. Hundreds of millions are devoted to

THE CZAR'S PLEA FOR PEACE. 205

acquiring terrible engines of destruction, which, though to-day regarded as the last work of science, are destined to-morrow to lose all their value in consequence of some fresh discovery in the same field. National culture, economic progress, and the production of wealth are either paralyzed or checked in development. Moreover, in proportion as the armaments of each power increase, they less and less fulfil the object the Governments have set before themselves.

"The economic crisis, due in great part to the system of armaments *à l'outrance*, and the continual danger which lies in this massing of war material, are transforming the armed peace of our day into a crushing burden which the peoples have more and more difficulty in bearing.

"It appears evident that if this state of things were to be prolonged, it would inevitably lead to the very cataclysm it is desired to avert, the horrors whereof make every thinking being shudder in advance.

"To put an end to these incessant armaments and to seek the means of warding off the calamities which are threatening the whole world—such is the supreme duty to-day imposed upon all States.

"Filled with this idea, his Majesty has been pleased to command me to propose to all the Governments whose representatives are accredited to the imperial Court, the assembling of a Conference which shall occupy itself with this grave problem.

"This Conference will be, by the help of God, a happy presage for the century which is about to open. It would converge into one powerful focus the efforts of all States sincerely seeking to make the great conception of universal peace triumph over the elements of trouble and discord, and it would, at the same time, cement their agreement by a corporate consecration of the principles of equity and right whereon rest the security of States and the welfare of peoples."

www.ingramcontent.com/pod-product-compliance
Lightning Source LLC
Chambersburg PA
CBHW020916230426
43666CB00008B/1470